Best
W's

DESTINY'S CHILD

THE UNTOLD STORY

MATHEW KNOWLES 2/29/20

DESTINY'S CHILD: THE UNTOLD STORY. Copyright © 2019 by Mathew Knowles.

Paperback ISBN: 978-1-9995825-3-1

Audiobook ISBN: 978-0-578-61848-7

TABLE OF CONTENTS

ACKNOWLEDGEMENTS

& DEDICATIONS

This book is dedicated, first and foremost, to all of the artists who participated in the journey of Destiny's Child, starting with Girls Tyme. Second, I would like to dedicate this book to all of the producers, writers, choreographers, road managers, music directors, business managers, video directors, engineers, dancers, band members, production crews, hair and makeup, attorneys, booking agents, independent contractors, merchandisers, tour promoters, and others. (My apologies, I know I've probably forgotten someone). Special thanks to Gia'na Garel whose writing, research, and gathering of the oral histories was a pivotal part of this project.

Lastly, I would like to dedicate this book to Arnie Frager, Alonzo Jackson, Debra Leday, Denise Seals, and Andretta Tillman who began this journey with Girls Tyme. Solange, who participated in many roles: sister, dancer, and writer. Tina, who spent endless hours as wife, friend, stylist, designer, mother (as well as bonus mother to Kelly), and was the glue that sometimes held them together. I would like to thank the incredible world-wide staff at Columbia Records, Music World Entertainment, Sony Music, and in particular Donnie Ienner, our strategic partners, and lastly, Beyoncé, Kelly and Michelle, who worked so incredibly hard for a dream that came true.

INTRODUCTION

For me, the phenomena that became Destiny's Child began with my own child—Beyoncé. The mechanics of managing, motivating, and maneuvering a group of talented children through an impossible landscape is one thing; parenting is another. Yet both had to succeed in this instance. Was that easy? Was it riddled with controversy and heartbreak, disappointments and finger-pointing? What do you think?

For my part, it all comes back to my personal role, and not only as a father to one of the group members but also as management. From the parenting perspective, I was not a pit bull fighting over a cash bone. I was a working father pushing for the advancement of his kid's nearly impossible dream. From the managerial side, I was leveraging their hard work as youths into a long-term advantage for them later in life. Because outside of the business of the show, there is still a legacy to be built. So it was never about getting richer. Money passed down is easily spent; it's the name the inheritors have to live up to, or not.

The group members built a name for themselves due to their talent and dedication. The name "Destiny's Child" and all its members are now renowned, and their inheritance from the hard work will be passed down to their children and their children's children.

Such financial success was beyond their young imaginations, but prosperity naturally came with being called "one of the most successful and greatest worldwide-selling girl groups of all time." That's also what you call a legacy. A mark on history that could even outlast money. Still, I figured if they would pass up college or a different career path for the sake of their art, then the financial and long-term career aspects should be considered. There had to be later rewards for all their early sacrifice. To risk all of that, and not have lasting security, would not have made any sense. I know this from my own entrepreneurial parents, as well as from seeing hardships that no father would want his family to endure.

From that business-minded upbringing, and my corporate sales and marketing background, I wanted to bring in not just the parenting but also the push. Not because it was *my* dream for them, but because they dared to dream at all and needed support. I wasn't alone, either. Others joined, adding to a sense of family and bringing even more progress to the movement of Destiny's Child.

The group's career launch happened during a freshly emerging era in black music, and it also ran alongside major changes in socio-political attitudes during the 1990s. We needed every sharp mind in the industry to pull off the seemingly impossible during those fast-changing times. It would seem from one point of view that black music and culture exploded across the globe in the 1980s-90s with rap, pop, and R&B. Yet on the industry inside, we would see how much had, and had not, changed since the early days of the music business.

Keep in mind, this was not one or two generations removed from the time when a young black woman's life wasn't even prized, much less her art—and certainly not in a multi-billion dollar industry. Whether you were a solo black artist or an artist in a group, your rights, royalties, and even your respect could be handled in whatever way that labels and backers wanted. It was seldom fair or pretty.

I knew enough of this treatment from having worked in Corporate America, and just by being a black man *in* America. I wasn't about to let these young girls enter into what was clearly a fixed game without help. Ironically, it was having a corporate career, during a heavily discriminating era, that later made such a difference with my strategies as a manager and a music executive. I was not always involved in many of the intricate early stages when Ann Tillman and others kicked off the journey. At that time, I was still working full-time as well as traveling a good deal, back when things had not yet crystalized into a structure that everyone could recognize.

Once it did formulate, nobody around the girls could miss it, and with Beyoncé at the core of the group's activities, I was going to be there, parenting if not doing more. By the time I joined Ann Tillman in managing the group, the girls were already in motion but needed a particular kind of steering if they were going to rise and crack the glass ceiling as a young, black all-girl group. Again, I can't emphasize enough how much it helped, my coming from a strong sales and marketing back-ground, top ranked for several years running. There, and growing up playing competitive sports, I learned the techniques of winning.

I knew, at the end of the day, we weren't selling the artists—we were selling their music and each individual's dream—worldwide. Once I did dig into management, I applied everything I knew. Where I wasn't, Beyoncé's mother was—and beside us there were others who dug in and gave their all to see that the talented children found their destiny.

Part of what I learned while building a winning sales team is that you need other people of vision to help. Despite any difficulties we might have encountered, in the end, we all seemed to maintain respect for each other's roles in the group's development. Nothing is taken away in our memories here. Not the early, much-needed efforts of Ann Tillman, Alonzo Jackson, Arne Frager, and Brian Moore, nor the production efforts of Daryl Simmons, Dwayne Wiggins, or Preston Middleton, nor the executive actions of Teresa LaBarbera White and Kim Burse, as well as the first team's roles played by Darlette Johnson, and vocal coach David Brewer.

Many of these players join me in these pages to relate, collectively, their memories about the early journey of such a hugely popular and ever-changing group. My own memories of the beginning, when I was still working full time, were further sparked when asking the early team members and those who worked during my own label's development, *"What do you remember?"*

What I remember the most are those early years that shaped Beyoncé, and even Kelly, because we spent family time as well as practice and show hours together. I also vividly recall what role I played in inspiring the group when and where I could. For example, there is one particular story I'll tell here of what was, for me, a pivotal point in Beyoncé's early life that may demonstrate why her musicianship is so startling: the memory of why she interprets songs from her heart and what I think made her a unique artist. Cultivating that gift was the least anyone who believed in her could do. Whether she was solo or in a group, working for a major corporation or as a schoolteacher, she was still going to be my daughter, with a dream that needed support.

Here, I will also speak in some detail about the other group members, the group's formation history, and provide a look behind-the-scenes. Then, other team players will fill in their parts. However, included here is also the point of view from a father's perspective and that of a family man. I offer insight that is uniquely my own, and give those who were just as necessary in their roles a chance to speak directly as well. There are many versions of how Beyoncé went from a pageant-winning child, (to be clear she only competed in the talent division) to a world-renowned superstar, not yet fully told by those who saw the first spark. Here, laid bare, is the group's evolution as told by the early landscapers of the music and the act behind Destiny's Child. There are the supporters of the dreams of girls too young to manage them within a business designed to keep those young black girls' dreams limited, anyway.

In this climate, Beyoncé didn't simply need her father; she needed a manager, a fighter, and teams of others who would also push toward—not just her individual goals, but also toward those of the group as a whole. It may appear from the outside to be a journey comprised only of synchronized notes and happy harmonies. However, there were screeching moments of pain for every single player involved. Even down to the executives and producers who gained so much ground, yet sometimes still lost ground after fighting hard for their vision.

It's a story that has to, at times, move from behind feelings and deeply personal moments in order to describe the importance of the actions, decisions, and directions taken to foster the group. This is more than just a view of my child, as I have to look back at the others who joined Beyoncé to form those harmonies that ultimately brought her out of her early shell. In music, she was in her element. Her passion had found a home and an extended family with her group-sisters. It is a journey with many moving parts and people. Helping to fill in sequences as they happened are some of the players, in their own words, sharing with me this oral history of the evolution of Destiny's Child.

Mathew Knowles, 2019
Houston, TX

1

ORIGINS

MATHEW KNOWLES

"You have to first understand that in our household, music was the fabric of every day, and every night. Especially the weekends. The girls were singing and dancing, and we were as a family watching Soul Train. We just had a love for music, similar to when I was a child."

DESPITE THE SIZZLING HEAT, I COULDN'T HAVE PICKED A better city to be driving around on a summer day. Houston, Texas, is where the first notes were laid to a musical journey being orchestrated by the hands of destiny. The town was special to me. Just like my passenger that day. In the backseat was Beyoncé, who was unconcerned about the heat because all she wanted at that moment was, "Daddy, can you turn the music up, please?"

At that young age, she was polite, soft-spoken, and obviously gifted. I glanced at her in the rearview mirror, thinking of how proud I was of her. Not just because of her talents, but because she'd developed them in spite of the obstacle of shyness, and often schoolyard-loneliness—things that had been worrying my wife and me around that time.

By then, word had spread around Houston of this little girl who was winning competitions all over the city. She had won about thirty of them at that point and was generating a buzz that had not been seen before from such a young, local artist.

For her and her sister, Solange, our household was not just a musical one; it was filled with fine art and entrepreneurial/activist parents who were already settled into middle-class life. At the time, I was working as the top sales rep at Phillips Medical System, selling MRI and CT scanners. Following that, and during the formative years of Beyoncé's career, I was a neurosurgical specialist with Johnson & Johnson. My former wife and friend, Tina Knowles and I, launched a popular hair salon called Headliners, which caught the industry by surprise with new and innovative marketing techniques, as well as unparalleled customer service. Tina was exceptionally creative and always ahead of the industry.

These were lucrative positions, and we were damned good at what we did, so life by the time my daughters arrived was well cushioned, some might say. Despite whatever racial or economic hardships we had crawled out of in our youth, Tina and I carved a solid foundation for our girls long before the singing started. Despite all of that padding, it was still harder than anybody might imagine.

For my part in the beginning, it mostly started on trips like these; coming from or going to some pageant or local event where Beyoncé's voice (and occasional dance skills) showed itself for all it was worth. It often brought trophies, smiles, and praises, and even surprise reactions that the little shy girl was the same one delivering such a powerful voice.

However, praise was not given to her everywhere she went— from the start she had detractors, if not outright haters, but back then, they were more in the form of teachers than peers or art critics. If she was going to receive the praise with the success; she also needed to understand the feelings of failure that came from hate, industry racism, gender discrimination, and even the economic racism that still threatened to hold her back. Tina and I had seen it, felt it, been angered and emotional about it, and fought against it. Those limits seemed like they were set on our community and could be seen through my car window when passing through Houston's Third Ward, and further out, where hope was even more desperate. As cushioned as my ride was, as comfortable as my daughter was with the music and the air conditioning, and her trophies waiting back home... I knew she wasn't getting the full picture.

I had the responsibility of getting Beyoncé back and forth to singing and dance practice, which, later, would be the same thing for Solange. At the time, I only saw these activities as an outlet for her to express herself and perhaps make some new friends, as Tina had suggested. My routine on the weekends was standard: grab her up, feed her, drop her off at practice etc., play basketball then pick her back up. That seemed to be our regimen, and I was pretty cool with following through. On this one hot day, during the typical routine of me driving her around Houston, when she was about seven or eight years old, we were just beginning to see her blossoming in those pageants.

Turns out, this day wouldn't be a typical ride. There was a defining moment that took place that gave me insight into young Beyoncé and the depths to which her love of music could take her as an artist.

When she was competing, she used to sing "Imagine" by John Lennon, and I wanted her to understand all of the words in the song because they're not insignificant. To make a point about the lyrics, that day, I drove her far outside of her comfort zone, out of the solid middle-class existence, away from the applause and beauty of the pageants.

"Where we going today, Daddy? I don't know where we are," she asked as I drove towards the outskirts of Houston. She had another performance coming up in elementary school and would be singing "Imagine" again. She had rehearsed that song over and over again at the house, so it was a natural selection for her competitions. Yet I could hear her in her bedroom almost searching for some understanding that she had yet to experience.

With her growing up on a side of town that had afforded her the better things in life—a life that was not necessarily privileged, but then again, not wanting for much—she was still limited. How can anybody deliver a message to the whole world one day and yet never understand who all makes up that world?

"Today you'll get a lesson on interpretation," I said. Of course she asked, "What's interpretation?" It was over 100 degrees on that afternoon. I turned the air conditioner off in the car and drove on, looking for a way to help her define the word by experience.

"Daddy, it's kinda hot. Can you turn the air back on?"

I had let the windows down to let her feel real air.

"Feel the breeze, instead. Beyoncé, air conditioning is a

luxury. Everyone doesn't get to experience being hot and turning on air to cool off. Sometimes you have to make the best with what you have even if it's not much."

To illustrate my point further, we drove to one of the poorest black neighborhoods in Houston, and I pulled the car up to a house where a family was sitting on the porch. I advised Beyoncé that I wanted her to pay attention to everything around her, and in the process make sure she spoke politely to everyone we met. We parked the car, had some water, and unannounced, went up to the family. We walked up on the porch and said, hello. I shared with them that she was my daughter and asked, "Can we just spend a minute with you?" Then we sat on the porch and talked to them, to see the kind of lives they lived and how difficult and challenging it was.

Houston heat is notorious, and anybody who has experienced it can relate to what it must have been like in a shotgun house with no A.C. running. I could relate to this because both Tina and I had grown up in shotgun houses, on dirt roads. The family was sitting on a porch because they didn't even have a fan —they were fanning themselves. The sofa on the porch was all worn and torn out, as were the chairs, and there was a hole in the middle of the floor, with a baby walking around wearing a saggy diaper and one sock. These were good people who accepted us into their environment, their home, and their family.

We set out after that experience to another side of town.

"Hello," Beyoncé innocently commented to each person we passed, while walking down the sidewalk. "Daddy can I help him push his buggy?" she asked of the homeless old white man pushing an old Food Lion grocery cart, probably full of the only possessions that he had left on this earth. The proud homeless man said, "Yes" with a tear in his eyes, and then Beyoncé did something that really surprised me and made me so proud; she gave the homeless man a hug and a kiss.

Finally, we went to a Mexican neighborhood and encountered a family celebrating a Quinceañera. They were surprised when we stopped and said hello. They quickly invited us into the backyard and offered me a beer, and a little girl grabbed Beyoncé's hand to join the party.

In the car on the way home I said, "Beyoncé, think about the lyrics of the song." At each one of these stops, when we got in the car, I would say, "Let's go over the lyrics. What part of the song do you think applies to what we just did?" She started crying when she understood, and that's what I had wanted her to do—understand. I wanted her to touch her soul, not just her passion for music. I wanted her to know that when you sing a song that was written with such passion and speaks with a message, that the only way to sing it and feel its true meaning is to know *why* the song was written and what it meant. I wanted her to put her own emotions and feelings into each song so that she wasn't just a singer but a messenger.

That day became a prolific moment in Beyoncé's life. If nothing else had changed, at least her interpretation of the song had. While practicing "Imagine" in her room after that, I could hear the difference from how she had sung it before. At least her interpretation of the song had changed. This would hone her ability to bring compassion and emotion, not only when singing "Imagine" but with every song she sang.

IT WAS TINA WHO FIRST RECOGNIZED BEYONCÉ'S GIFT. SHE and the girls would be cleaning up around the house, and Beyoncé would sing while doing her chores. The more Tina paid attention, the more she realized the normally shy and quiet little girl truly had another side to her. She really could sing. I remember Tina telling me, "It's like she becomes another person when she sings! I, mean, who would've thought that a mature sound like that could come from such a small little girl?"

When Beyoncé was five years old, she attended a Catholic Montessori school where I played a critical role by getting on the board. There, I worked hard to make sure that the arts were covered—we always put emphasis on art. I knew that was where my kid's love and passion was, and I devoted myself to it while I was on the school committee. We purchased a mixing board for recording, microphones, and new speakers so when the kids had presentations, we could hear them. There's nothing worse than going to an elementary school event and you can't hear the kids —especially after they've worked their hearts out. It shouldn't be because of the technical side of the program that the audience can't enjoy it.

From the start, it became a habit to try and supplement whatever creative moves my kids made, doing whatever would help them succeed at it. When talent seems born into children— without any influence or support from their parents—it is a force everyone instantly recognizes. Beyoncé had that, and even if her mother and I had done nothing, I'm certain it would have risen out of her in time because it was unstoppable.

Recognizing talent, even when the children are young and shy and unable to find a voice in the world, much less one to pour into a microphone, makes you fight for it. You may as well get behind it early and give it steam, because their inner passion for art is not as quiet as their mouths might be. I say that because for Destiny's Child, with Beyoncé as a member, to become such a bold group, it's incredible because I watched Beyoncé and Kelly starting out as such shy kids.

For example, with Beyoncé, at school, I would pick her up on most afternoons after class because I had flexibility with my job. Sometimes, I would also take her to school in the mornings. When I would go there, it would sometimes be sad, watching her. She wouldn't at first see me while swinging in the school-yard, alone. The other kids would be in other areas, playing, and she was there, isolated. I used to ask, "Well why don't you play with the other kids?"

Her answers were usually the same: "They don't like me," or "They don't understand me."

I'd be sadly trying to figure out ways to make her happier. I can only imagine that perhaps Michael Jackson and other musical prodigies might have been just like this. These special, talented kids ... their left-brain/right-brain processes are different.

Beyoncé was always in a creative space. An inward place reserved for music, images, and future dreams far bigger than those of the average kid's. That's where she always was when she was alone—in that space. It's the inner world of the artistic, creative type that makes them different, because the talent is huge inside a young person's limited body. They can't let us inside, and they haven't developed a way to share it all yet. That has to be a struggle.

In later years, she would become a musical icon with millions of other kids who looked up to her, but before any of that was foreseen, she was just a child wanting to fit in. Unfortunately, sometimes kids, and even teachers, can be cruel. If Beyoncé's name came up in a conversation about those emotional bullies, my response would usually be, "Fuck them damn kids! They ain't gotta like my kid! She'll be okay. They're just jealous!"

As parents, you want to shield your child from all the harshness of the world, and you never want to hear how your baby, who only shows love towards people, is not accepted by some of her peers. The effect was that by them not warming up to her, it caused her to be more introverted. I used to want to get her out of that as a parent, and that's why I would always say, "Beyoncé, tell me what it is you love to do?"

The word "passionate"— children don't quite understand that word at that early age when it comes to their dreams. Yet that is what she was for the arts, and she could only describe it as, "I love to sing; I love to perform." For a girl of few—and of the few—soft-spoken words, she chose the ones she used deliberately and with meaning. It was real for her, not a plaything or just something to do. It was her passion, and Solange would follow soon in her footsteps. What is a parent to do?

Well, to support that, we surrounded Beyoncé with the tools. We got vocal and dance coaches lined up at a young age. To follow, would be those numerous pageants. Tina and I enrolled her in talent competitions to help her overcome her shyness. Not only did Beyoncé beat out her competition, she began to observe the mistakes that others would make around her, and she learned from them. Soon, her air of confidence blossomed. This was despite people who subtly, if not outright, tried to deny her gifts, to hold them back or hide them, or otherwise limit her.

She had teachers who never supported her dream. Unfortunately, there are a number of teachers, especially in elementary school, who just don't understand the arts—period. They don't understand kids who are different or who have this incredible talent that they thrive on, which is part of their purpose. Beyoncé was no different from a lot of young people today in elementary and middle schools; she had teachers who didn't support her art at all.

In the second grade, her teacher was talking to me and saying, "Beyoncé needs to spend more time on her math than singing."

I replied, "I'm very pleased that Beyoncé made a C+ in math because I know she gave it her best. So, as long she gave it her best, I'm happy."

Another time … she was in the seventh grade, and there was going to be a school play. Beyoncé Knowles, who was one of all of these little kids growing up, buzzing throughout the community grapevine as a rising star … who had won all these awards … and the teacher in charge of the play still gave her a role as a tree. We were livid about that choice but understood the dynamics of it. This was a predominantly white school—a scattering of black kids. I simply said, "You know what, just be the greatest tree ever." That's how I always talk to my daughters. Regardless of what it is, be the very best at it and give it your all.

By the time she was beginning these competitions and traveling with her singing, her greatest thrill was going to see Michael Jackson when she was five or six years old. No one could know that one day, she would be admired by and even similarly compared to him regarding her rise to success. She worked hard for her craft from that day on. The other art forms followed and ran alongside her vocal growth, as when she joined a dance troupe.

Darlette Johnson, Beyoncé's first dance teacher, played an extremely pivotal role. When Beyoncé was six and seven, Darlette's dance troupe would travel all over Texas and compete. They would be the only black dancers doing so at that level. They were competing against wealthier white dancers that had tons of money, great outfits, and their music was perfectly arranged. Here were these little black kids, who were competing against all odds. Even when their music was cut off in the middle of a routine and wouldn't transition, they made it work, with Beyoncé often the lead dancer.

One time there was a category that was called Song and Dance. Darlette said, "You know, Beyoncé can really sing. She's always singing."

I replied, "Well I know she does around the house all the time." Darlette had her mind made up and told me, "I'd like to put her in the category where she can sing and dance at the same time." So Beyoncé did that for the first time—and won. That's when she got really excited about being able to dance and sing as a performer.

I focused on my parenting role and carrying out the things that I think all parents should do, including listening to their kids' dreams for their lives, and then surrounding them with the means to help them accomplish them. That's what I've done with both Solange and Beyoncé from the start.

Once Beyoncé got into dance deeply, we started looking for a vocal coach for her so she could work on her range. Soon enough, she was getting better and began competing all over the city, and then all over the state of Texas. Her confidence grew with her wins, and her exposure revealed what could be accomplished if she pushed herself.

One time, where I saw this fully emerge was when Tina and I, along with Solange (who couldn't have been any more than three years old), were at one of Beyoncé's competitions. It was time for the judging to begin, and we were just waiting for the results.

"I'll be glad when they give me my trophy and my $100," Beyoncé said. I looked at her and asked, "How do you know you won?"

Her reply was simply, "I just know I did."

She actually did win that competition. So there it began. She would gain valuable knowledge with every performance that she put on and apply the confidence behind her faith in her gift. Eyes were watching, and people were noticing.

You have to first understand that in our household, music, singing, dancing, and fashion shows were the fabric of every day, every night—especially on the weekends. The girls were singing and dancing and we were, as a family, watching *Soul Train* together. We had a love for music, similar to when I was a child and my mother and father would dance to the records I spun as the "house DJ" … always on Sundays after dinner. For Tina and me, ours was an art-filled household full of black pride and cultural awareness, as well as song. Once Solange turned four years old, she also got the talent bug and loved dancing and singing. So I had these two kids performing around the house all day long—and actually sometimes competing against each other.

Eventually, Beyoncé began to venture out. We got her into all of those pageants, even though I actually hated them. I didn't get what making little girls dress up to look twenty and thirty years old was about, and I didn't like it. I didn't like seeing that. I said that if Beyoncé ever got involved with that, that she could never do anything other than the talent part, and Tina agreed with me. Neither of us wanted our kids doing that. So Beyoncé would only compete in the talent portion of these pageants, and she would win every time. Winning set a precedent for her at a young age. She had the stuff to achieve beyond any set limits if she stayed consistent. What she needed were not just the tools, but we all needed a team to take her to the next level. Who knew that it would come out of those early competitions, where so many eyes were watching? Eyeing her there one day was dance instructor, Darlette Johnson, who, with many others, helped shape what was to become Girls Tyme.

2

GIRLS TYME

Darlette Johnson
Dance Instructor

I BEGAN TEACHING BEYONCÉ DANCE WHEN SHE WAS ABOUT six or seven years old. She was such a quiet and shy little girl. Her demeanor was always so pleasant and innocent, you couldn't help but love her. I remember one day when we were at my studio, and she was the last child to be picked up. I was tidying up, when she leaned down to take her shoes off and started singing. Automatically, my ears came to attention. What was this I was hearing? There's no way this little girl was singing, "Been Around the World" just like Lisa Stansfield! I asked her, "Wow, can you sing that again for me?" But Beyoncé's shyness kicked in. So I said, "I'll give you a dollar if you sing it again," and of course, like any little kid with a dollar in hand, Beyoncé began singing the song.

"The whole world is gonna know you!" I told her.

"They are?'" she asked.

In all my excitement, I told everything to Deborah LaDay. I explained to her that I had a student she had to see perform. I informed her that Beyoncé had a performance coming up at the Evelyn Rubenstein Jewish Community Center. Deborah had a business partner named Denise Seals, and when it was time for Beyoncé's performance, both ladies attended. It started everything from there.

MATHEW KNOWLES

After Beyoncé's performance, Deborah and Denise made their way through the crowd to Tina and me. They were totally blown away by Beyoncé's talents and were on a mission to make her a part of the all-girls revue that their company, D&D Management, so desperately wanted to form. What was ultimately the first introduction of some of the girls who would later form Destiny's Child (after many incarnations) officially started with their efforts. Within a short time, Ann Tillman joined the management team.

At that phase, they were Girls Tyme, and they began working with producer Alonzo Jackson out of Oakland, California. Brian Moore was one of the writers. This was also the beginning of a rollercoaster ride of girl group names that would be used as the girls performed and gained notoriety. Girls Tyme, Somethin' Fresh, Cliché, The Dolls, Destiny … there were so many group names and just as many girls who joined—a revolving door.

The two original members of Girls Tyme were Beyoncé and Staci LaToison. Then came Kelly Rowland and Tamar Ashley Davis, which made up the singing portion of the revue. Millicent

LaDay was the "hype girl" among them. The hip-hop dance element of the group, called Girls Tyme, was made up of LaTavia Roberson, Chris Lewis, and sisters, Nicki and Nina Taylor. Denise served as the vocal coach for the group, but during downtime, Beyoncé, even at eight years old, directed the girls with their harmonies and showed her leadership abilities.

"Make sure you sing it like this so that we're in harmony and sound good," I recall her saying one evening when I was sitting and waiting for rehearsal to be over. At that time, my primary focus was on my daughter, but all of the girls had something special about them that made them stand out.

Most people don't know of the talented young Latina girl in the group, Staci LaToison. When Girls Tyme first started, she was about ten or eleven years old. She shared lead vocals with Beyoncé and was dedicated to the group by always giving 100 percent at every rehearsal. She has her own memories of that time and where her journey ultimately took her.

Staci LaToison
Member of Girl's Tyme

WE PLAYED TRUTH OR DARE, HIDE AND GO SEEK, AND danced around, but mostly we dreamed of being singers. If we were at Beyoncé's house, Solange would be right there, trying to join in with everything that we were doing. She was about three or four years old, and she was so cute and so typical the "little" sister. We were your quintessential girls' group, except we had additional elements with dancers and rappers, and for the most part, all the girls were really good friends and got along great.

During that time, there were a lot of musical groups that had a male influence such as Another Bad Creation (ABC), Boyz II Men, Kris Kross, and New Edition. My mom felt that the various boy groups had such a strong presence on the music scene that she thought we needed to stand out as girls, so she came up with the name of our group, Girls Tyme. Mom felt like it was time for the girls to shine! And shine is what we did!

It's so funny … when looking back on those days, we only had one or two original songs; we mainly sang other artists' songs. Beyoncé and I both were lead vocals at the time, and I would sing "Hold On" by En Vogue, and Beyoncé would sing "Hero" by Bette Midler. Even back then, at an early age, I can recall that Beyoncé sang with so much emotion. She really had a presence about her.

Things seemed to be going pretty smooth at that point. We would put countless hours into rehearsing, and all the girls and the parents had a definite dedication to making sure the group was successful. Shortly after that is when I started feeling like there was a shift of attention … maybe some favoritism. It started somewhat subtly but became quite obvious later. During that time, management had changed slightly, and we were managed by Andretta—"Ms. Ann" Tillman. Ms. Ann was initially brought in to help with financing us, then she eventually became our manager. Denise and Deborah were still around but didn't have much presence once they asked Ms. Ann to step in. By that time, Ms. Ann was working with a small staff that included Alonzo "Lonnie" Jackson.

The late hours were wearing on me, and then I started noticing that the producers would call Beyoncé in to sing when we first arrived at the studio, allowing her to sing while her voice was fresh. Me, on the other hand, I was always called into the studio at three and four in the morning to sing after I had been napping and waiting on my turn to get into the booth.

Most of the time my voice was scratchy, and I took a minute to adjust because of the wait time involved. I was a kid and was doing everything I thought I was supposed to do to remain a team player. That's until the producers started bullying me and acting mean towards me. It was as if I couldn't do anything right. As a kid, and constantly feeling like I was being criticized by the producers, my confidence and self-esteem started being affected.

This lack of confidence eventually trickled down to my schoolwork. I was normally a straight-A student, but because I felt like I needed to impress the producers and everybody else, my main concentration branched away from making sure I maintained my grade-point average to focusing on the group.

I would show up just like the other girls and give my all, but I really felt like the producers showed favoritism towards Beyoncé. I remember one time when I felt like I had been sabotaged. It was a night when we had a show, and everyone in the group who was singing solo had performed before me. When it was my turn to sing solo, my back track didn't work. Now, I can't say that it was truly done intentionally, but just by speculation I felt like it was done on purpose because it coincided with the way I was treated when we were in the studio.

Shortly after that, my parents and I both started noticing that there were so many girls coming and going in the group, and that management was becoming very disorganized. My grades started going downhill, so my parents came to the conclusion that it was best for me to leave the group. They wanted me to get back to my main focus, which was academics.

MATHEW KNOWLES

At this point it seemed like changes were part of the norm. Hotels, per diems, airfares, and tutors for the girls started becoming very expensive, and so, drastic changes needed to be made. Andretta Tillman—A.K.A. Miss Ann, was the main person in charge then and pretty much controlled how things went. She would sometimes make sure it was known that since she had the money—she made the rules. Couldn't anybody argue or be mad at that! Lonnie was still handling the producing, Brian Moore was still writing, Darlette was doing the choreography, and Tina, the wardrobe. Everyone had a role and carried it out with professionalism and dedication from the jump.

Andretta's friend Kenny was brought in to assist her, and then one more addition to the group was added, David Brewer. He was brought in as a vocal coach and was great at what he did, which was making sure the girls' harmonies were together. He also made sure the girls' vocal exercises were done correctly and that discipline and focus on their craft of singing was maintained.

Linda Ragland and her sister were the first booking agents, and they handled the merchandise for Destiny. (*An interesting coincidence here*: Linda Ragland actually has a flyer that has Jay-Z and Destiny performing in Jackson, Mississippi. He was the headliner, and the opening act was the girls. Unfortunately, the show was canceled.) So Linda goes all the way back, since she helped during Girls Tyme, then became my general manager at Music World Entertainment for four years when the group's name was Destiny.

Within the girls' revue, changes would still be taking place.

In fact, there were constant and sweeping changes happening throughout the group, as well as in our household. It affected everyone, from Tina and me, on down to Beyoncé and eventually, Solange.

All of that group growth happening so fast and furious had some impact on Solange, who was seeing her big sister get all this attention both at home, outside of the house, and at the dance studio. Solange always would do things that would get your attention that would say, "Hey, look at me."

I remember coming home one time, and I don't know where Beyoncé was, maybe at practice or something, when Solange had been left with the housekeeper. When we got home, Solange had dismantled some of Beyoncé's trophies. Some of them, we couldn't put back together. But it was her saying, "Look at me. I exist as well." I can better understand it as I've gotten older. The importance of those moments when Solange was trying to get our attention, well, we can all agree she's gotten the world's attention now as a singer, songwriter, Grammy-winner, and fashionista.

These were parenting sidelines, unseen to everyone else, yet this demonstrates how the process of driving toward one kid's success so early can have an impact on the siblings. It took a balancing act of knowing we had two powerful talents under one roof, and while one was making her way through the maze of success, the other was equally needing the same nurturing—in her own way.

When the next set of changes occurred—family- and group-wise—it was with the discovery of Kelendria "Kelly" Rowland, who joined the group as a backup singer. Kelly was a compelling talent, yet bashful and very unsure of herself. She had a beautiful voice, could sing, would constantly stay on key, and her tone was always on the money. She and Beyoncé hit it off almost immediately. They became best of friends and still are to this day. While their connection as friends was developing, and just as the group began establishing a bond, a change in Kelly's life would transpire. Her mom, Doris, worked as a nanny for an affluent white couple, both of whom were doctors. She and Kelly had living quarters at the couple's house.

One day Doris's boss came to her with no advance warning and told her that changes were being made and that she and Kelly would need to find somewhere else to live within thirty days. Doris wanted to go back to Atlanta, which was her hometown, but she wanted to have her act together so that she could properly take care of Kelly. She saw the potential that Kelly had with being a part of the girl's group and the closeness that Kelly had, not only with Beyoncé, but also with our entire family. Tina and I sat down with Doris, and the three of us decided that Kelly would stay with us for thirty to sixty days while Doris got things together in Atlanta, then Kelly would eventually move with her.

As time went by, it became obvious that Kelly really enjoyed being in our house, and Doris soon realized that her daughter was very committed to the group and that we loved her and would treat her right. That's exactly what we did. We treated her as if she were our own child and constantly made sure that she knew she was loved. She had living arrangements that she had never had before. From staying in an affluent black neighborhood in Houston, to her own sisterhood of experiencing constant fun, and simply being able to enjoy being a child. She ended up staying with Tina and me for over twelve years.

As a young girl, we're talking eleven or twelve years old,

Kelly was so caring and sweet that she never made any waves with anybody. She was always a team player and naturally humble. She appeared grateful to be able to live with us and never gave us any disciplinary problems or any problems at school. Problems at school? I talked to her Spanish teacher in high school, who thought it was okay to bully Kelly in class. I remember coming home to find Kelly crying her heart out. The next day, I went straight to her class and gave that teacher a tongue thrashing. All of the students applauded, and I just remember Kelly with the biggest smile on her face.

Kelly was always a good person—that was who she was by nature and anyone could tell. She appeared shy and quiet because that's the environment she was often in that cultivated that. Her mother, being a nanny, I could only imagine, was more subdued in that atmosphere, living in a home with white affluent doctors and kids. So when Kelly came to us, that's who she was.

She always had a love for Whitney Houston. That was her favorite artist, and she had a voice similar to Whitney's. She worked extremely hard, but what stood out for me was that she was just really shy. I can't overemphasize that. But then, Beyoncé was also. The difference is, when Beyoncé got on that stage or in rehearsals, that shyness was 100 percent gone.

As Kelly got older, she started dating, and as she lived longer with us, she gained more confidence. Tina and I never looked at Kelly and saw any differences between her, Solange, and Beyoncé. We never said, "Well, what we do is going to be different with Kelly than with our own kids." It was never that. We never even thought of it that way. We were a family, and she became part of it. She called me Dad, and she called Tina Mom or Miss Tina. So it was that type of environment. It did impact her, because it must have given her stability, and the group more confidence.

They would all need it—that confidence. Soon they would be leaving the state more often and spreading out. They were being looked at by established producers and players in the industry. After Kelly, next to join the group was Ashley Davis. Her personality was the complete opposite of Kelly's, but she definitely was a wonderful addition to the group. She was outgoing and very seasoned vocally for her age. She was an excellent singer and had an incredible vocal range. In comparison to Beyoncé, Ashley had a more mature voice that didn't quite match that of an adolescent. Her voice was strong and adult-like, in contrast to Beyoncé's voice, which was still continuing to develop in both tone and vocal range.

One thing that really stood out between the girls was that when it came to stage presence, Beyoncé was the stronger of the two. Beyoncé could capture the audience without hesitation, but there was no doubt Ashley's voice was stronger, overall. However, Ashley was larger and taller and stood out from the group.

Even as the group continued adjusting to new tactics, newer members, and group names, other players, including me, would soon have to make major adjustments as well.

By 1991, the owner of The Record Plant Studios, Arne Frager, was interested in recording with the girls and requested that they fly out to Sausalito, California. This was a major move, as Arne had worked with numerous legends in his studio, like Ella Fitzgerald, Chaka Khan, Prince, and Santana just to name a few. Money had become tight so everyone wasn't going on this trip...just Andretta, Kenny, Brian, and the two lead singers of the group, Ashley and Beyoncé. During that trip, recording at the legendary The Record Plant Recording Studio, a major development would take place that would alter the course of the group's direction and lead.

Arne Frager
Producer, Sound Engineer

THE RECORD PLANT OPENED IN 1971. IT WAS ACTUALLY A division of Record Plant Los Angeles. It was a kind of get-away studio that I took over and became the owner of in 1988. So it had quite a legendary history in the '70s, before I got there. Prince did his first record there, "For You." Rick James recorded, "Super Freak" there, and Whitney Houston also did her first records there. Many artists recorded at The Record Plant long before I took ownership of the studio. But I had to rebuild it because it had been basically shut down for almost two years. When I took it over, things were not doing so well. I restored the studio, keeping some of the original glamour.

Before Girls Tyme arrived, I had a number-one hit with Michael Jackson in 1983 with a group called Rockwell: "Somebody's Watching Me," which was an artist development project of mine where nobody paid me, and nobody brought me the group. I had to go out, find the group, and put the record together, and Girls Tyme was a similar thing.

I was very interested, in the early '90s, in finding and developing new talent. There were a number of what I would refer to as "little boy bands" around at that time. A good example would be New Edition and one called Color Me Badd. As with the Jackson Five, all the bands had four or more members, and they were really young people who were doing well. There was a huge push for youth and boy bands in the early '90s.

I had worked with the guy in Los Angeles who produced Bobby Brown, Lou Silas, and I told him, "I'm going to look for a little girl band," and he agreed that was pretty good idea. So I started telling everybody I knew that I was looking for a young female group of girls that really had some talent that I could work with. Because my business plan was always: find a group, sign them, record their album, and then shop that to record companies. So I was on the lookout for a group like Girls Tyme, until I heard about them and contacted their management. I got on a plane to Houston and went to Mathew's house, where the girls held their regular rehearsals in a nice-size room.

The girls did an audition for me live at Mathew and Tina's house. So that's how I found them. But it wasn't something anyone brought to me. It was a situation where I was looking, and I was actually going to find four individual girls and put together a band. But when I found Girls Tyme, they were already a six-girl unit. They already had a lot of material, so they were just perfect the way they were. I was very excited and made them an offer that they accepted

They were pretty raggedy and not as polished as a '60s group. They certainly needed a lot of work, but they had a lot of work already under their belts too. You could tell that they were really into it. It wasn't like anybody was twisting their arm. But of the six girls, I think there were two that really stood out. When you're looking for a group that's going to have hit records, you realize that success depends on more than the records—it's got to be a group that can entertain on stage. In that group of six were two who stood out. One was Beyoncé and the other was LaTavia. Those two had the real outgoing personalities that you could immediately recognize. Even at eleven years old, a person could say this one could be a star because she just had this kind of shine to her. To be honest, Beyoncé certainly had that, and so did LaTavia. I did a couple of music videos with the girls, and one was done in a shopping mall that featured just those two.

At that time, it was Alonzo Jackson who mentioned to me, "Oh, I know, I know of a young girl act in Houston, they're pretty good." So because he knew about them, and he had some relationship with them, I was able to meet them. There was another young man by the name of Tony—more of a songwriter or lyricist.

They were already working with the girls, so when I decided to sign the group. I thought it would be comfortable for them to work with someone they were already familiar with. So I formed a company with Alonzo, and we co-produced the record under the auspices of a production company called Arne and Alonzo. It was formed just for the purposes of that album. The choice of songs to be recorded was made by me and Alonzo together.

We're based in Sausalito, and the girls came here and stayed in a Holiday Inn Express, in a city called Mill Valley, which is adjacent to Sausalito. Because Beyoncé and Kelly were about the same age as my daughter, whose name is Mara, she invited them to come and stay at our house. They came, and had a sleepover, but they stayed in a hotel for the most part. They had with them one of their managers, Ann Tillman, and I believe there were maybe one or two other women. I didn't know how they were involved then, but the one that came with the six girls was Ann Tillman, along with Lonzo and Tony.

We picked the songs and I think we recorded about an album and a half of the songs we selected. Almost all of them featured Beyoncé because we wanted her to be upfront in the group. We also kind of felt, when we listened to the songs, that she really had the better energy. We had some guy we'd hired to do a video of the BMI showcase, where we featured the girls performing, and I wish the guy had his shit together because the girls were great. Beyoncé was adorable. It really would be a great video that we had, but it's really grainy. It's not good enough to show what I mean about that shine in her then.

Every day, they'd come over. I sent my company van to the Holiday Inn Express, which was about ten minutes away, to bring the girls over with Ann Tillman, and they'd work in the studio. Mostly they were there to do the vocals because the instrumental tracks were just a bunch of drum machines and synthesizers, and we did those before the girls came out. So we had the instrumental tracks, and we asked the girls to come do the vocals. Because all six of them were there at this time, I was able to put on the live shows as well as shoot the two videos.

Everybody was together for close to a month or more. I dealt with Mathew and nobody else after we made the record. I had a number of deals to go out there and place the record and get it sold. Because over the years, I've learned that signing a group and making a great record with them is only about one half of the battle, or even less than half. I have been pretty good because of my background in sales, which is something Mathew and I had in common.

I was pretty determined to get the girls a deal. So at the time

I was working with them, I was also working with Prince, with whom I'd had a twenty-year relationship as a recording engineer. So I talked to Prince about the girls and I sent him, at most, three songs. I don't know that I sent the whole album because usually it was my practice that less is more, so I probably only sent him the three I thought were the best.

Prince called me up and said, "I love this. These girls are great! I would love to sign them. I have my own label so I'm very interested." {*Author's Note: Later, Ashley as Tamar Davis signed with Prince and became his protégée.} So I was very excited about that. Then I had another situation after that, which was also very promising. There was a woman named Suzanne de Passe.

Suzanne was very famous in the record business and in the TV/film industry. She was the right-hand woman, so to speak, to Berry Gordy, who could convince him to sign *this* band, or don't sign *that* act. She was basically at Motown to help groups get their stage act together. But she wound up being very influential with Berry, and one of the groups that she told him to sign was the Jackson Five, when he didn't want to sign them. He didn't think they were anything special.

So Suzanne got the credit for signing Michael Jackson to Motown Records. Then she went on to produce television shows. And she did a series on cable, *Lonesome Dove,* a TV series Western that she produced, and it was a big deal. Very successful. Suzanne had a management company in Hollywood, and I sent them the tape. They got ahold of someone that I had known up in the Bay Area that used to live up in Oakland: Ruth Carson. Ruth called me up, came over, and met the girls, and she said, "Look, I work for Suzanne de Passe Management, but I'm a manager under Suzanne. We have a couple of people that handle the day-to-day, and I want to sign these girls. I think they're great. I think they're going to be big stars."

I said, "Ruth, this is, this is great!" because I knew who Suzanne was and what that could mean. I knew that as a manager, she could get them any record deal anywhere because she was a heavyweight. I thought it was going to happen with Ruth Carson.

Literally, a week or two later, she called me up and told me she had just been offered a job in New York as VP of Marketing for Sony Music. Off she went. That was the end of that. Neither one of those things happened. Prince never followed through, and Ruth got a job. Then we booked the girls on *Star Search*, thinking that there was no way anybody was going to beat them. I mean, it was just impossible, they couldn't. I thought that would help them tremendously because *Star Search* was a big TV show offering a lot of exposure. They went on *Star Search*, and I thought they performed very well. Then the group they were up against won for some reason. It was a great, great disappointment to the girls, and I wasn't too thrilled myself, obviously.

MATHEW KNOWLES

I'll interrupt Arne here to interject what I was seeing going on during that *Star Search* episode. It, after all, is what sparked my interest in stepping in fulltime because of how it turned out. It was after that show that I began working more with Ann Tillman, who actually still had a partnership with Debra and D&D Management. Thereafter, Ann and I became partners exclusively. At that point, it was the original members. When I say original

—even before I got involved, Girls Tyme was a revolving door of probably at least ten different members. Even my niece, Angie Beyince, was once a member. But again, when I became partners with Ann and co-managed, it was Beyoncé, Kelly, Ashley, LaTavia, and her two cousins, Nikki and Nina, as dancers.

So from my perspective of this time ... Shortly after their California trip to record, as a gesture to show that he believed in the girls' singing abilities, Arne booked them on *Star Search*, which was the equivalent of *American Idol* now. It was the break that they had been looking for. With this type of national television exposure, and by winning the competition, the girls would have not only made $100,000, but would have been put on Front Street in the entertainment world.

It was to take place in Orlando, Florida, to be shot in November, and then was scheduled to air in February of the following year. Preparations started immediately. Tina started making costumes for the girls, and constant rehearsals were taking place at every opportunity available. Beyoncé had never lost a competition before, so her mindset was that they were going to win. "Daddy, we're gonna be so famous, but I'm kinda nervous a little," she told me. Still, I had never seen or felt that Beyoncé had a doubt about winning, after all, she had never lost any competition. Even so, that was a lot of responsibility for a little girl who was going to be singing the lead for the show. Previously, Lonnie, Andretta, Brian, Kenny, and I were all debating as to what song would be the best choice for *Star Search*.

I felt like they needed to sing a ballad to show that the girls could really sing. I suggested, "Sunshine", which to me was appropriate for the judges to see their talent—even if Ashley was singing first lead and Beyoncé was singing second lead. That wasn't as important to me; what was important was that they won. They were already at a huge disadvantage with five older white men judging, and the girls competed against a rock band of thirty-five year olds.

However, Andretta, T-Mo, and Kenny wanted the girls to sing "Boyfriend," and Lonnie and Arne wanted the girls to sing "That's the Way It Is In My City,", which included some rapping from LaTavia and Ashley.

To me, it really didn't make any sense because you were looking at a bunch of older white men who were judges, and at the time, the only rap that was out was gangsta rap. If we could've waited to do that same song the following week, I thought we might have been okay because Donnie Simpson from BET was going to be one of the judges on the next episode. I felt like the rest of the group had no clue as to what they were doing.

"Old white men can't associate with that shit! They're gonna look at the girls like ... what the fuck is that?" I argued. However, the consensus was to go with the song that Lonnie and Arne featured, and it featured Beyoncé so I went on and agreed.

When it was time to travel, we packed so much shit that you would have imagined that we were moving to Orlando instead of simply visiting. I remember when we arrived at the airport and I was pushing carts and carrying bags... there were so many freaking bags that when we checked into the hotel, we had to purchase another room just for the damn bags. So there we were in Orlando, and the moment had come for the girls to face their challenger, which was a rock band out of Chicago, Skeleton

Crew. It consisted of roughly four to five older white men who looked like they were about thirty-five-years old.

They put on a nice rock band performance, but they never actually played their instruments—which to me seemed odd. Most rock groups actually play their instruments when they perform, but this one didn't. The girls were up next, wearing their beautiful costumes that Tina had created. They put on a good performance, which could have used a couple of improvements, but overall it was a good, solid performance. Not great, but good. I don't think the girls were comfortable with the song. Something I would come to learn later as a manager is that their comfort with a song is important to a performance. Skeleton Crew received four stars and Girls Tyme received three stars.

While the girls were on camera, they kept their composure, but by the time they went backstage, the crying started like water flowing through a river. Beyoncé took it the hardest because she had won all of her competitions before joining the group, and a loss was something she had never experienced. It hurt me to see the girls hurting. I loved each of them so much and to see them feel disappointment really crushed me. I went up to Ed McMahon and asked him what type of advice he gave parents who have children that experience a loss on his show. He said that he never quite understood why the people who consistently won on *Star Search* never went on to professional success.

In his deep and pronounced voice he explained, "Actually the people that consistently win on the show don't have a successful professional career, however, the ones that lose, like Boyz II Men, Usher, and others that went back and changed their organization, refocused, and recommitted, became stars. They basically improved on their skillset, refocused, recommitted, and then went on to become quite successful."

That's when I decided to get involved with fully helping the group. It was a defining moment for me when I became a manager to their careers and not just an observer.

Shortly after *Star Search*, Girls Tyme would continue to make changes. There was a noticeable physical change that was taking place with Ashley, for starters. She began to develop more quickly than the other girls. Looking at the group perform on stage, they appeared imbalanced, mainly because Ashley was taller by a couple of inches and looked much older than the other girls, even though she wasn't. It didn't help that her mom was constantly fighting with management about her daughter being the main lead and not playing second to Beyoncé or sharing lead with Beyoncé.

Then, Ashley Davis, Kelly, and Beyoncé were the vocalists. But we had to make an immediate change once Ashley's mother —and I understand a mother loving her kid—expressed she was unhappy that Ashley wasn't the lead singer. She thought that my involvement now, being a co-manager, would be supportive of Beyoncé even more so, and that Ashley would not be the lead singer. But Ashley had simply outgrown the other girls, as kids do. In a group, you don't want that. You want symmetry and a kind of a similarity in weight and height. Imaging, especially with a girl group, is critical in the music industry. This would play itself out, soon enough.

Meanwhile, we had to make some decisions with the dancers, and ultimately, we let Nina and her sister go. I'll explain the record business logic behind that coming up. The most significant change was LaTavia, moving from dancer to member of the final group. She always had this wonderful personality, star appeal, plus she had the looks. At that time also, she had some notoriety in that she was on the cover of this kid's product called Just for Me. So she had some degree of fame in that, which played into the decision as well.

I had flexibility in my job in sales, so I could pretty much do my own scheduling. One of the things that happened when I first became co-manager with Ann is that we did a number of team-building exercises. One that we did (I learned this from working at Xerox) is that I took the four girls—that would've been LaTavia, Ashley, Kelly, and Beyoncé—and I got a book for each one of them. A hardback book. I put it on the carpet in our den area. They all lined up on one end of the room and were told to scoot on the book along the carpet.

So the exercise was, *how do you get everybody to the other side of the room? If somebody touches the floor then that person has to start all over again.* That was the only information given. The girls all lined up; they were anxious, excited, and I said, "Go!" It was interesting because Ashley immediately started scooting as fast as she could to get to the other side. That was an indication because the answer to the drill is: We all get over together. So you literally scoot the books and one person lines it up, one person steps across, and then the other person steps across until everybody gets over. It showed, psychologically, that Ashley was really about herself and not about the group, but she was also right: she has done well as a solo artist. I've used that exercise a number of times since.

Once LaTavia became a member of the group, we had to replace Ashley. At this point, we needed a vocalist because that was not LaTavia's role. Imaging was a part of it as well. The height, the shades of color, the size, all of that played into the imaging of what would ultimately be Destiny's Child.

There was a search we did in Houston with an audition. A number of girls came to our home. Beyoncé was a part of the audition process, from just a creative side, giving feedback on how she felt about the vocals. At this time, Beyoncé was around the sixth grade, going to middle school. There was this girl at the school who also came in and auditioned, and that was LeToya. LeToya had a bubbly personality, good voice, and good energy. After auditioning maybe fifteen girls, the decision was made to bring her in. When you bring in any kid, you also bring in their parents. That always becomes a challenge with any kid group. You not only signed the child, but you signed the adults; not on paper, but fundamentally.

ASHLEY DAVIS EVENTUALLY ENDED UP LEAVING THE GROUP because her mom felt that she wasn't singing lead enough and that her talents weren't being fully utilized. After even more revamping, it was decided that there was no longer a need for a rapper or dancers, so Nikki and Nina were cut. However, LaTavia was not only beautiful, she was charming and had an engaging personality, so we made the decision to make her a backup vocal.

So, this was where Beyoncé, Kelly, LaTavia, and LeToya started together. Little did I know that these days would lead to a magnificent collaboration among those four talented girls. Their journey would be a storybook tale that would be the music history CliffsNotes© used by many artists and musical acts that followed.

I make no excuses for who I am, and the devotion I carried and still carry for my girls. When I began analyzing how management was being run and the importance of the success of the group, with Beyoncé being one of the key factors, I felt that it was in the best interest of the group for me to become more involved.

I went from being the dad who dropped his baby off at rehearsal and then played some hoops, to a dad who was now a co-manager with a vested responsibility for the group. I had done so by boldly approaching Andretta and telling her that I wanted to be co-manager and if she didn't want to agree I would understand, but then we would just pull Beyoncé, and possibly Kelly, from the group and manage her by myself.

As much as it sounded like an ultimatum, it was just a simple fact. If Beyoncé's presence was important enough in the group, then I was going to make sure I assisted. Even if Beyoncé had to leave the group, she still would have been successful because I knew that singing was her passion and what she was destined to do. Whatever she wanted to do with her life I would have supported it. Hell, if she wanted to be a doctor, I would have found a way to buy her a hospital.

With me coming onboard, there was hesitation from Andretta, and rightfully understood. She didn't know my capabilities nor my work ethics, but the biggest thing she wasn't aware of was my determination. I never thought on a small scale, nor did mediocrity ever surround me. I was then, and still am to this day, a creative and strategic thinker, but beyond all of that, I was a father who loved his daughter and would do whatever necessary to make her dreams come true.

So now, moving forward, Andretta agreed to a 50/50 co-managerial role for me, which brought up the issue of Denise and Deborah.

Denise was a good person, but the relevancy of her being in a managerial role was unwarranted. Deborah, on the other hand, was a live wire who was constantly battling with me over petty shit. It wasn't gonna work out with her for the simple fact that she and I didn't get along. It was because of this that Deborah decided to leave altogether, and I was happy with her decision.

Since I was now co-managing the group, I felt it would be best to have the girls' rehearsals closer in proximity to where they lived, so I decided we would have rehearsals at my house. I wasn't gonna lie though, I truly wanted to be more hands on, and so, having them at the house allowed me to have more input and influence. I even went as far as building a stage in the backyard for the girls to rehearse on.

I was dead-ass serious when it came to them learning and developing their craft. Once I'd made my decision after *Star Search*, I had a directive. At that phase, Kelly hadn't started staying with us yet because this was before her Mom was relocating, so she would get a ride with Andretta, Ashley lived close by, and LaTavia's mom just brought her over without any difficulties. The girls were on their grind and the bond between the four of them was undoubtedly strong. Darlette was still the choreographer and was always on point with making sure the girls knew their routines, despite any challenges.

Darlette Johnson
Dance Instructor

ALL THE GIRLS WERE PRETTY GOOD DANCERS, BUT KELLY, Lord have mercy ... bless her heart, she just couldn't dance! Beyoncé would dance out of her costume if you let her, but Kelly would struggle to learn the routines. One thing that I will say though, is that the girls would help each other. They weren't gonna let her fall short, so they assisted her in learning the moves. Eventually, dancing became second nature to her just as it was with the other girls. They were truly a team, and Mathew made sure of that. During rehearsal, they wouldn't be done until he said they were done... not until "things were done right!" I remember him telling them, "You are only as strong as your weakest member." No, Mathew, didn't play!

MATHEW KNOWLES

Even before *Star Search*, Arne Frager began lining up even more opportunities for the group while adjusting it. Major changes took place the day after they arrived in Sausalito when everyone was at the studio. Lonnie (Alonzo Jackson) had been trying to get Ashley to execute the sound that was needed to pull off a quick tempo, a syncopated song that T-Mo had written called "Blue Velvet." Ashley was having difficulties with the song, and although she was a great singer, everyone was becoming weary because it was taking too damn long for her to get the song right. Beyoncé had been sitting back, observing, and was running the melody in her head like a scientist on an experiment. Her excitement in feeling that she could execute the song couldn't be contained. She looked at Kenny and told him that she could sing it. Kenny told Lonnie, Arne, and Andretta that Beyoncé felt like she could sing it so he suggested that they let her try. Lonnie had a fit because he had spent a long time coaching Ashley with the song, but Andretta convinced him that enough time had been spent on Ashley, and it wouldn't hurt to see if Beyoncé could do it. With that said, Beyoncé pulled a trump card. Her tone and ability to adjust her voice to the unexpected rhythms blew everyone away. She totally impressed Arne with her newfound talent, and he felt she had just taken things to a whole other level.

T-Mo had written the song and was in total awe of her execution and articulation of his body of work. From that point on, the lead was no longer viewed as a shared position...it belonged to Beyoncé solely.

It was almost a mutual decision when Ashley left the group. We had learned that Arne Frager had gone out to a lot of record labels, and they had told him, "Look, one of the reasons we don't want to sign these girls is you have three girls and you have four dancers, that's seven people. Then you've got parents, which is another ten people. That's seventeen people that we got to deal with. We don't want to deal with that."

Arne and Ann were trying to, literally, sign the dancers to a record deal with Ashley, Beyoncé, and Kelly, which is unheard of, having dancers as part of the record deal. So the decision was made. I mainly forced the decision that we needed to make a complete change in the organization in terms of management, which we did, with Ann and me. Arne continued to play a major part in pushing the group through this new phase—with Ashley

as lead, and faced challenges in getting others to come ride the
wave.

Arne Frager
Producer, Sound Engineer

WITH THE GROUP, WE ALSO DID A COUPLE OF SHOWCASES
sponsored by BMI here in San Francisco, in a rented room
downtown called Demos. It was a very well-known nightclub,
actually. Formerly a speakeasy in the '20s that's been in San Francisco ever since. It was a beautiful little room so I rented it quite
a bit. The girls' showcase with BMI was well attended there. Still
we faced problems getting them to the next level, despite how
talented they were.

I was involved in a possible partnership at that time with
Ralph Simon, who founded Zomba Music and Jive Records.
Ralph planned to leave the record company and move up to the
Bay Area to start a new one where he and I were going to partner. I told him to come to the show, thinking, "We'll sign Girls
Tyme to our own label and put them out ourselves because he
has a lot of money. (Ralph left his company with probably fifty
million in the bank)." So I said, "Ralph, we could start this
company and sign this group easily." So he came to that BMI
showcase.

He said to me in his British accent, "I think that Beyoncé
could be a star!" An eleven-year-old! He looked at her, and like
me, we both saw a star. Yet what did he do? About a month later,
after telling me he hated L.A., he took the job as Senior VP and

Operational Head of Capitol Records in Los Angeles, so he moved there and that was the end of that.

So I was disappointed by all these series of near misses, but I kept at it for quite some time. For example, one of the relationships I had at the time was with Sylvia Rhone when she was at Electra. Sylvia told me, "You know this is really good, and I think the girls are good, but you've got six girls plus twelve parents. Most of the parents are divorced, which means for us to make a record deal with your girls we have to deal with twelve attorneys."

Wow. "Well I don't think they're all divorced," I tried to argue, but she said, "Well, it's a very complicated deal, and we gotta have contracts ready and ratified by the court for girls under twenty-one. It's just too hard. There's too much money involved. We pass."

Basically, every other record company passed. So I worked on that issue, not just in the studio, but after we finished the record. I was the one who took the record everywhere because I really believed that we had something, but nothing happened. I understand that at some point Mathew took over and started doing the managing full-time

Sometime early to mid-1992 is when Mathew started really pushing. My relationship with the girls was not as manager, it was producer. Now, as producer, and having the girls signed to my record company, I didn't have to go out and try to shop them for a deal because that's usually a manager's job. But it was something I did for every unknown group that I worked with, and I was used to going around. So all the record company people knew me because I was making hit records for them.

So I didn't ever think of myself as a manager of the group, I always thought of the managers as Ann Tillman and Mathew. I didn't know until much later that Mathew really wasn't their manager in the beginning until eventually he saw that somebody needed to take the reins and move things forward, and he was the guy for it.

I always thought Mathew was the right guy for it even though I was far removed from the politics of what they had to deal with, between him and the ladies in the original management company. I can tell you this: I always saw Ann Tillman as kind of like a den mother, someone who was not going to really be able to interface with the record industry and move things forward. But she was someone who was going to watch the girls when they came to San Francisco, kind of as a chaperone, and as a mom. She was a wonderful lady, and I really liked her. But I think if Mathew hadn't taken the reins and really made it happen, it wouldn't have happened.

I think the most significant things that I was able to contribute, besides trying to present the group to everyone in the industry, were two-fold. One, the group as it was presented to me had the lead singer as Ashley Davis—and she was a very good singer, actually, for her age—but she was a little bit larger than the other girls were. She was the biggest of the six since most of them were pretty small.

I expected that Ashley would be a good singer, but not in the front line. I didn't see her as a person who could front a group. She didn't have that kind of personality, and from my point of view, Beyoncé sang quite well and had that spark. Beyoncé, if I'd be honest, had the personality. So I insisted when we started doing lead vocals that she become the main lead singer. I found out later that that was somewhat controversial within the group.

I didn't know that. I mean, nobody argued with me about it, but they had all sort of wrapped around Ashley as the lead singer. However, I just didn't think she was going to move the group forward. I thought Beyoncé had an energy and a certain shine that you have to have as the front of a group. So I think that was a pretty important change that I made to help them. Then, the other one is, I was producing with the group, Tony! Toni! Toné!, at the same time the girls were at the Plant. Because the Plant has four studios under one roof, it is like it's a multiplex studio. You'd have Rick James in one room, Prince in another, and Sly Stone in another. Since that was the kind of place it was, we had a lot of big stars at the studio all at the same time.

So we had The Tony's (as they're collectively called) working with me in one room, or maybe they just came by to hang out because they heard about the girls. They met the girls while I was working with them, and later on with Dwayne Wiggins, who co-founded Tone Tony Toni, and is the person who helped them as the group, Destiny's Child, get signed to Columbia Records.

I wasn't there for the signing of Destiny's Child. I wasn't involved at all with that phase. But I think that Beyoncé and Kelly met Dwayne at the Plant, so I asked Dwayne about that. He said, "Yeah, that's where we heard about the girls first." But it was much later that Girls Tyme broke up, and Destiny's Child got formed that they came to work together.

3

THE DOLLS

MATHEW KNOWLES

Daryl Simmons
Songwriter, Producer

ANDRETTA AND I WERE GETTING THE GIRLS BOOKED AT various spots around Houston. We wanted everyone to see their talent, so when the opportunity to book them for the Black Expo came, I jumped at the chance. I was able to get them on one of the "B" stages, which basically was one of the smaller stages for lesser-known talent. Prior to their performance, numerous demo tapes and publicity materials had been sent out on their behalf to various record labels and music executives.

One such producer/songwriter, Daryl Simmons, received a call informing him that he needed to check out a young all-female group from Houston that was very talented. He was advised that a tape would need to be sent to him, and if interested he would take it from there. I was informed of this and immediately sent out the VHS tape for him to review. Daryl viewed the tape, loved the girls, and wanted to see them. I advised him that they had an upcoming performance at the Black Expo in Houston, which worked out perfectly because his wife at the time was from Houston, and he agreed to fly out.

Daryl Simmons was close friends and business partners with Antonio "L.A." Reid and Kenny "Babyface" Edmonds. He had grown up with them back in Indianapolis and later worked with them with various mega-stars such as Boyz II Men, Toni Braxton, and TLC through their production company, LaFace Records. Daryl was a silent partner with L.A. and Babyface and had his own production company called Silent Partner Productions ... hence the name. His production company had a newly formed partnership with Elektra Records, and he was looking to sign some new artists to his roster.

To clarify the difference between a production deal and record deal: In a production deal, the artist is signed directly to a production company, which makes the album then turns it in to the record label. When an artist is signed directly to the label, they work directly with the staff, specifically the A&R (Artists & Repertoire) who makes the record. The artist or the artist's management is involved with the label in all aspects involving production and marketing and any other aspects of the artist's career.

In my opinion, it would be a strategic move if Daryl signed the girls. After all, he, L.A., and Babyface were like brothers, but they were still very competitive with each other. With L.A. and his wife Pebbles having a girl group, Choice, with lead singer Pink on the roster, and Babyface having TLC on his, it just made sense that the girls were the ideal candidates to join Daryl's roster.

On the stage at the Black Expo, the girls performed in front of an audience of just a handful of people. It wasn't a full audience, but just as I'd told them numerous times before, "Whether you're in front of fifty people or fifty thousand people, you always need to put on your best performance."

In the audience was Daryl and his wife Sherry. They were both impressed with the girls and wanted them to come back to their hotel to see them perform again and to discuss business with me.

I told the girls of the opportunity that was in front of them, who Daryl Simmons was, and about the artists that he worked with. They were so excited and thrilled. Their eyes were big as saucers as they jumped up and down, anxious to meet him. "I can't wait for him to see us up close," Beyoncé yelled.

When we arrived at the hotel, Daryl greeted us and offered snacks, and then the girls performed a ballad named, "Sunshine." The song I had wanted them to perform on *Star Search*. Instantly, he was in love with the girls, their talent, and their enthusiasm.

We were still grooming the girls in Houston, with constant rehearsals while strengthening their vocal skills when we received the call from Daryl that he was signing the girls and wanted them to fly to Atlanta. Although it took him a minute to sign the girls, the news was like a kid opening gifts on Christmas Day. We were all ecstatic. Daryl wanted to start working with the girls immediately and requested that they fly out so that he could learn their voices and personalities.

When they arrived in Atlanta, they were assigned tutors and were temporarily assigned to two producers to assist with production: Tim and Bob. Their assignment was to start producing songs for the girls, and then Daryl would critique the work afterwards. At that time, Daryl had a huge workload and was tremendously busy in the studio, producing such acts as Monica and SWV (Sisters With Voices). His production partnerships with LaFace Records, LA Reid, and Babyface, allowed him to work with such luminaries as Boyz II Men TLC, Tony Braxton, and others.

As Daryl spent more time with the girls, he could hear, during studio time, that Kelly was not nearly as developed as a singer as he'd like. When he made it known, Beyoncé would step in and say, "Give her a chance. Just one more chance."

"Beyoncé was very selfless in that way," remarks Daryl. "She was the best tool that the group had because the other girls couldn't sing as good, but my main goal was to produce the best record possible even if it meant that only one person was singing all of the parts."

It was also at this stage of the game that Daryl's wife, Sherry, stepped in to assist with grooming the girls. The first suggestion that she had was to change the name of the group to The Dolls. She had some ideas on how she wanted to style the girls, which would soon backfire and cost Daryl a lot of money.

Shortly after, Daryl decided that he wanted to put on a big showcase that would feature the girls. He had invited quite a few heads of record labels and producers to the showcase and was looking to get as much exposure as possible. He was hoping to generate a huge buzz about the girls so he invested a lot of money and time in putting the showcase together. He also wanted to include an act from his hometown of Indianapolis, which at the time was KeKe Wyatt. According to Daryl, KeKe was terrified about performing on stage and refused to sing for the showcase, even though Daryl saw this as an opportunity for her.

She had an extreme bout with stage fright. On the other hand, The Dolls were ready to excite the crowd, but when they performed, they did just okay … perhaps even better than okay but there was a huge distraction to their performance.

It was their outfits. Sherry had chosen to dress the girls in '70s themed outfits that seemed more appropriate for adult women than little girls. Hip hugger pants and shirts that were tied at the waist to show their stomachs … it was such a distraction that no one paid attention to the actual performance of the girls.

"The audience simply couldn't get past the outfits, and on numerous occasions, stated that the girls were too grown and too sexy. They were too risqué and showed too much skin," states Daryl. He felt that with groups such as Kris Kross and their trendsetting "clothes backwards" look, and TLC with their hip "hat to the back" baggy clothes look, that the girls were going against the grain and bucking the system by wearing such outfits.

The reviews for the showcase were awful. "No one, I mean, no one liked the girls," Daryl commented. He had spent a lot of his own money meticulously putting the showcase together and making sure that everything was on point. It was an unfortunate loss to have the girls' talents go unnoticed because of their attire.

A video of the show was recorded and sent out to notable bigwigs in the music industry such as Puffy, Clive Davis, Babyface, and even Arsenio Hall. But according to Daryl, none of them liked the package. Daryl would go on to say that Jheryl Busby, a big-time music executive at Motown Records, loved the girls' performance but simply wouldn't give him the deal that he was looking for. The showcase turned out to be unproductive.

"Shortly after the showcase, I remember LaTavia asking me, 'Why we not signed to LaFace?' " says Daryl. He states that he felt that if he had the girls sign with LaFace Records, they would be shelved. He also mentioned that The Dolls were his first production deal and that he was young and inexperienced and this was his first of everything. "I should have signed them to LaFace, hands down. That's what I should have done," comments Daryl. "L.A. liked them and Pebbles liked them."

Pebbles really wanted them. I remember her saying, "D, c'mon, let me have them." Years later, after the success of Destiny's Child, Beyoncé flew Daryl to New York to ask questions pertaining to her documentary. The question was raised as to what happened with The Dolls.

He reminisces about the four hours when he sat talking with Beyoncé while advising her that The Dolls was his first endeavor. He wasn't trying to rely on the names or status of his famous partners. He was trying to stand on his own because everything he had done previously was mainly through LaFace. "Sylvia Rhone of Elektra flew down to Atlanta to an empty space to see The Dolls perform, along with a rap group and a solo artist. I was looking for a three-act deal," states Daryl.

"Between my workload and the paperwork to get the girls signed, it seemed like it was taking forever, and Mathew was becoming very impatient. So impatient that he began calling Sylvia directly. He was getting frustrated because things were not moving fast enough," Daryl declares. "I was getting frustrated with Mathew because he didn't know music like I did, but looking back on it all, we both had egos and we both wanted our respect. We didn't feel that either of us was getting the respect that we deserved, and that's where things began to sour." Sylvia eventually pulled out, and the Elektra deal was over.

Daryl had grown to love the girls and cared deeply for their well-being. He had spent a lot of time with them so when things didn't come to fruition it was a hard situation for him.

"I'm a true believer that things happen the way they're supposed to happen. Beyoncé would have been successful, regardless. As a matter of fact, I wanted to name the group 'Beyoncé.' I was into one-name groups like Van Halen, and I thought the name Beyoncé was so different and creative, but Mathew said that the other parents would kill him," he laughs.

"Me and Mathew may not have always seen eye to eye but one thing is that we both knew the girls deserved a record deal. I admired Mathew and his business sense and dedication. To parent managers like him and Brandy's mom and even Joe Jackson, I have to give credit where it's due because they identified (long before the world knew) that their kids had talent ,and then they sacrificed everything for their success. With Mathew, at that time, I may not have liked everything that he did but in the long run I have to give him respect because he did it his way."

4

CLICHÉ INTO SOMETHIN' FRESH

MATHEW KNOWLES

To RECAP, BEFORE WE GO ON TO THE NEXT INCARNATION AS a group: First, it all started with the management company of Debra, her partner Deborah, and eventually, Ann Tillman. At that time, they were Girls Tyme, and they were working with Alonzo Jackson out of Oakland, California. Alonzo Jackson was a producer, Brian Moore was one of the writers. Alonzo found Arne Frager, who owned the Record Plant studio in Sausalito, California. Arne Frager and Alonzo Jackson formed a company called A & A Music, and then A & A Music signed Girls Tyme. Alonzo and Arne were the producers and writers.

When Daryl Simmons found the girls, they became The Dolls. He was the only exclusive songwriter and the producers he had assigned Tim and Bob, were producers and songwriters in Atlanta. They worked under him in his company Silent Partner Production. The girls became The Dolls, and they signed to a production deal with Daryl Simmons and Silent Partner Productions. Silent Partner Productions then did a production deal with Elektra Records. So that's the order.

When that deal ended with Daryl, the girls came back to Houston. There was a minute when we had to stop because Beyoncé had really worn out her vocals. When they were The Dolls and they were in the studio, Daryl really leaned on Beyoncé to do the lead vocals as well as the background vocals.

As said about that phase when they were The Dolls; Daryl was somewhat disappointed, at times, with Kelly. So Beyoncé had to carry the load of the group vocally. When she got back to Houston, she had really damaged her vocals and we had to take her to one of the top vocal specialists in the country, which we were lucky was here in the Houston Medical Center.

There was a period of about three months during which Beyoncé didn't sing and didn't talk unless it was a necessity. She was on vocal rest for that period, and we were all really frightened that she had damaged her vocals in a way that she would never be able to sing the same way as she had before. We were very fortunate and blessed that didn't happen. So during the period of the group's incarnation as Cliché, she was mostly on vocal rest. But they still worked on the choreography.

As Cliché, they met Preston Middleton here in Houston. They were in the studio working with Preston on a number of songs, but we only used one. But they were in the studio for months, working with Preston after the deal with Daryl and Elektra Records went awry. While in the studio with Preston, they did an amazing cover of "Wanna Be Where You Are" by Michael Jackson.

Once we changed the name to Cliché, I sent out a number of packages to the record industry. In those packages there would be a bio, a couple of songs, and photos. We got a number of responses back, where record labels passed. At this time, the girls were just really in artist development mode.

Once I got all of those letters from the industry saying that they passed—and these were major record labels like Atlantic, Capital Records, and others—I came up with this idea that, looking back, wasn't a good one; it was a poor idea, but I thought, "Okay, I'll change the name, and I'll resend these packages back out. I'll just add a new song to it with a new name: Somethin' Fresh." But that didn't work. That period of Cliché and Somethin' Fresh, although it covered about a year, was only a short period in their long career. About six months with Cliché and six months with Somethin' Fresh.

The girls performed one of the songs they recorded during this period on *Star Search*. It was the wrong song, called, "All About My Baby" that was nationally televised. Again, it featured LaTavia rapping on the song. But the most notable song they did during this era, a song that we will use as the single when we launch this new album of Destiny's Child (that's never been released and was recorded in 1992 when they were Girls Tyme), is "Sunshine." It's a beautiful, beautiful ballad.

Eventually, the many name changes and group fluctuations would become stable enough for real success to take over. It seems once we locked in on a name and the right members, what was to be their ultimate destiny entering the charts came as Destiny's Child.

We were looking for a name when Tina went to the Bible, and something dropped out on a page that was a marker in the Bible. Her eyes went to the word "destiny." So that's how the girls went from Somethin' Fresh to Destiny. There was a period when they were simply named Destiny. In fact, they were signed to Columbia Records as that, but we got a cease and desist letter over it. Turns out, because there was a female gospel group in Mississippi that was named Destiny; we had to change that name quickly—within twenty-four to forty-eight hours. So my thoughts were, "Do I put a name before Destiny or after the word Destiny?" and I just decided on Destiny's Child.

During this period, when they were still known as Somethin' Fresh and on the verge of being Destiny's Child, the girls did a video called, "I Can't Stop" with Lil' O. Now, on YouTube you'll see it as "I Can't Stop" Lil' O featuring Destiny's Child. It started out more like this....

HOUSTON IS NOTED FOR ITS UNIQUE RAP ARTISTS. IT WAS A rap era, mind you, but not for everybody. Many had yet to see that genre of music as it's seen now. I might say I was one of them, at first. You see, ironically, the first record deal ever offered to the girls was when they were still being called "Girls Tyme." It was Rap-A-Lot records, one of the largest rap labels in the world, founded by James Prince back in 1987. They had a division that was called Sing-A-Lot.

James actually gave me a contract and told me to fill in the blanks. I was a little concerned due to the reputation of the artists at that time in the rap industry. I didn't understand it completely then. But I was involved in the community here in Houston, and in the industry, you couldn't be involved back then and not be associated in some way with rap and hip-hop.

I built a relationship with the owner of Rap-A-Lot, who to

this day is a friend. With such introductions, I met an artist at a seminar where he performed, and I talked to him about his music, and eventually, I signed him to my management company. That was Lil' O, and with him, before I ever did deals for Destiny's Child—in any of their incarnations—I got a record deal at MCA Records when it was the elite urban record label in the world. They had Mary J Blige, New Edition, Puffy, Jodeci, Heavy D … and that's a pretty stellar lineup just to name a few.

So that was my first indoctrination into the music industry, in terms of managing artists signed to a major record label way before Destiny's Child.

Since Somethin' Fresh, Cliché, and even Destiny were names the group used for such a very brief period, it's understandable how some can think they came in as Destiny's Child—later they were, and thus the association with them under that name when referencing the Lil' O, "I Can't Stop" video. Nobody hardly knew them as Somethin' Fresh or Cliché. But by the time Lil' O's first single came out, the girls were then signed to Columbia Records as the group Destiny.

Then I, from a strategic standpoint, thought of bringing the girls onto his project in some way. His song had a chorus in it, so I asked that the girls sing it, and if they could also be in the video. So if you go to YouTube and pull that song up, you'll get to see the first video that Destiny's Child—as a group they'd begin to be known as—appeared in.

I WAS DETERMINED TO MAKE SURE THAT THE GIRLS HAD everything they needed to be successful, to get to the next level.

One decision that Andretta and I made was to change the name of the group. Since the loss on *Star Search* had been such a huge one, she and I decided that it would be good to start with a new name for the group, just to give things a clean approach. We came up with the name Somethin' Fresh. By changing the name, we both felt that it would give the girls the opportunity to focus on moving forward while concentrating on their craft and not dwelling on a loss.

There was one more decision that I felt needed to take place. David Brewer was still their vocal coach at the time and an excellent and structured teacher to the girls. In order to constantly work with them without any outside disruptions, and with him agreeing, I decided to move him into the garage apartment that was attached to our house. That way he would have full access to coaching the girls' voices at all times, with the biggest emphasis on coaching LaTavia. She had come from the premise of being a dancer/rapper and wasn't really a singer, but she brought an element to the group that was definitely complimentary. In order for her to keep up with the other girls, vocal coaching was needed.

From there, rehearsals became a boot camp of sorts. I remember studying singers, seeing them perform while huffing and puffing on stage, and sounding like a hot mess because they weren't trained to sing and dance at the same time. I was going to make sure that didn't happen to the girls. So while doing choreography, which was already a vigorous task, the girls would sing.

While keeping them physically fit and on a strict diet, the biggest test in keeping their voices aligned with their movements was to have them jog and sing at the same time, as well as rehearsing in high heels. Later on in their careers, this would be something that people noticed and took heed to when grooming their artists.

Of this period, Darlette recalls a funny side to the boot camp memories.

Darlette Johnson
Dance Instructor

Mathew was strict on the girls when it came to their diets and didn't allow them to eat fast food. I remember there were times that Solange would be around, and just like a kid sister, would come back and tell me if Beyoncé snuck food from Burger King. Solange was like a hall monitor, but if you asked Beyoncé if she ate the food she would always admit to it. She would never lie.

THE BOOT CAMP TRAINING WAS BUILDING THEIR LUNG capacity, and it was also building their stamina, because as we all know now about Destiny's Child, choreography and dancing were a critical part of their routine. You break the group into the dynamics; its dancing, vocals, imaging, and media presence—but especially the vocals. And vocally it has always been that the harmonies are so different and distinctive.

When you hear Destiny's Child's songs and you hear the harmonies and the melodies, you immediately know it's them. Then there's the image; imaging has always been a critical part of Destiny's Child. Tina played a major role in the girls' imaging. The other part is media training and team building, and it's a critical part, which is why they didn't implode, as many girl groups do. The main thing in the beginning for me was the conditioning and stamina to take it psychologically and physically. Because if you think about it today, the girls of Destiny's Child were athletes.

To be able to dance and sing for two hours almost nonstop, except for a minute, minute and a half, wardrobe change, requires the same amount of stamina that it would if you were a football, basketball, or tennis player. Even in football, you've got a defense, you've got an offense, you've got substitutions. In basketball, you've got substitution. It requires more stamina because you're running up and down. Except in tennis, it's just you and it's you that whole match, moving. I understood that, so those were all the steps that we worked on, very hard.

We would jog on the bayou in Houston. The girls would sing and run, and I would be with them. I wouldn't be able to do that today, but I could then! Ultimately, we built a stage in our backyard so they could rehearse out there and be in real show condition. I bought microphones and karaoke equipment so we could have the music without the vocals. We made those investments at an early age. I started this early in their careers. Once official rehearsal was over, Kelly and Beyoncé would do their routines on their own. I never individually worked with the girls at home. Once at home in family mode, there were no rehearsals. I was out of artist management mode and back to father mode.

There were times when Kelly and Beyoncé, on their own, would go upstairs or outside and work on stuff. Yeah, that happened. But it wasn't because it was a supervised and organized rehearsal. Beyoncé was always driven at a different level than all the girls, including Kelly. She was always driven because this was her passion. It was all the girls' passion, but she was just driven in different ways than any of them. I say that, and I can understand that because I've always been like that. Tina's always been driven. So Beyoncé saw both her parents at it very early.

I fundamentally think that children are pretty much developed by the time they're seven or eight years old. They're pretty much 75 to 85 percent of who they are going to be for the rest of their lives. In her early development, with Tina and my successes, Beyoncé saw her parents driven, along with Solange and Kelly.

I do get annoyed and I do get insulted sometimes with comparisons of me to Joe Jackson. As if I forced this dream on them. Now I did some research, and there are some actual comparisons between the Jackson family and the Knowles family. Those comparisons are (some of this was even interesting, and I had never known): The Jacksons' mother, Katherine...up until I did my research about a year ago, I didn't know... when her boys were the Jackson Five and very young, made their outfits— similar to what Tina did. So there are some comparisons between Katherine Jackson and Tina; it was the creativeness and the imaging aspect of it. Katherine was sometimes the glue that held the group and family together, and I can say the same about Tina.

Joe worked in a steel mine, a blue-collar worker. Joe was a musician and actually was in a band. He'd had aspirations to get signed to a major record label himself. That was not my background whatsoever. I was fortunate to go to college, grad school, and eventually earn a Ph.D., and fortunate to work in corporate America, and fortunate to perform at extremely high levels in corporate America. I went back to school to understand the record industry. I took artist management classes, production classes. I took classes on songwriting and publishing and went to an array of seminars around the country. When I got into the industry, I had, at least, some fundamental knowledge from a business perspective. Joe Jackson loved to go into the recording studio with the kids. I hate going (and still do) into the recording studio, as well as video shoots. That is not something I like doing.

I think I've spanked Beyoncé once in her life, maybe twice, and Solange, maybe four times, maybe five. The youngest always gets the toughest love. I've never hit my kids like Joe is said to have done with his. Yes, we punished them, but I've never been physical with my kids, as has been described about Joe Jackson. Not even close. The few spankings my kids got were when they were like two and three years old, for doing something they shouldn't have been doing. Not when they got older. We wanted to teach them accountability.

Tina didn't work for six years after we got married. Beyoncé was five and Solange was two before she went back to work. She was too gifted to sit and just let things happen around her and not be involved in her own dreams. I asked her, "What is *your* passion?"

She said, "I love styling, designing, and hair."

I said, "Well, why don't you go to cosmetology school, and once you get your degree, we'll open a hair salon."

I had that same fundamental kind of belief in Solange and Beyoncé. I wanted them to live their passion. Tina wanted them to live their passion, and she too was passionate and driven.

I would have been just fine if they had wanted to be an attorney, lawyer, hairstylist, whatever they wanted. As long as it was their goal, not mine. Theirs. That's a big difference between the environments that these two families lived through. When it comes to being *their* dream and *their* drive not yours, you'll see the difference between myself and Joe Jackson. I would have never been like that. What was always key for me with Solange, Beyoncé, and Kelly was that, if you aimed low and made it, versus aiming high and missing, I would be okay as long as you aimed high and gave it your very, very best.

THE TEAM WAS NOW FORMING, WITH MYSELF, ANDRETTA, Lonnie, T-Mo, Kenny, David, Darlette—and Tina was making the girls' outfits. Everything seemed to be falling into place until Andretta began having issues that were weighing heavily on her. She had been faced with some unfortunate health problems, but she still gave 100 percent when she could. I knew that the girls needed as much exposure as possible, so I would look for every opportunity to let them perform.

Tina felt the same way, and since she was the co-owner of a successful hair salon in Houston, she figured the girls could perform periodically at the salon while clients were getting their hair done. Looking back on it, it kind of reminded me of the intro to Eddie Murphy's *Raw*, where he would perform for the family when he was a kid, and everyone would encourage him. It's kind of how the ladies at the salon would sit back and coax the girls. "They shoal can sing and dance!" they would say. "Tina, what ya'll gonna do with them girls? They talented!" Now you see the creative behind "Bills, Bills, Bills" video.

Yes, indeed. The girls were talented, but they needed to know more than just singing and dancing if they were bound to be successful.

Dwayne Wiggins
Musician, Producer

WELL, MY EARLY INTRODUCTIONS, IN THE BEGINNING, would have to be when I think Beyoncé was around nine years old. I believe the name of the group was Girls Tyme at that time. A friend of mine let me know that this was the group he was working with from Houston, Texas. There were about six members, if I'm not mistaken. I didn't get a chance to meet that group, but I do remember Beyoncé sitting in the backseat of the car, with him and his co-producer in the front, telling me how good they were.

About two years passed, and I was working with a few other groups when I happened to be at my studio, and I saw a picture on the wall of Girls Tyme. I said, "Whatever happened to that group right there? I remember you were telling me about them." My buddy told me, "Oh they're working with Daryl Simmons or something."

Then I got a call about a month later (my buddy had turned my number over to Mathew).

"Hey, my name is Mathew Knowles, I got your name from my partner, Ann Tillman, I'm interested in talking to you about working with your label."

I had a little production label at that time called Boom City. I did a few deals, you know, with some majors like Universal, that at that time was called Polygram. I had my lines there, and I had some dope management. I had managers that were managing Meat Loaf and Duran and Richard Marks. A lot of pop groups, and I think the Tony's were more of the urban to that. We were doing pretty well.

So I think when I look back at it now, I think that's probably one of the only reasons Mathew Knowles would want to deal with me because I had organization around me. I had organized people around me. I was a studio rat at that time.

Mathew said, "I'm really interested in working with you."

I said, "OK, what's the group?" I had never really heard any of their material.

He sent me a cassette, and I put it in. About a minute and a half or two later, I listened to this voice. I had to call him back. I was like, "Hey man, I ain't stupid. These ain't no thirteen- and fourteen-year olds, man!" He kept saying they were kids, and I was like, "OK, whatever. All right, so tell me how you want to move, because I know that's not no kid."

He says, "No, no, let me show you the VHS." I remember sitting at home and putting that tape on, and I saw them sitting on stools just singing.

I was like, *Damn. Whoa! Blown away.* I mean, I liked it. I liked the rawness of it, and the fact of the matter is, they had their own styles. You could hear it in the voices. Even when Beyoncé talks. You could hear that southern tone. Sorta like Aretha Franklin strong, the way her voice is. That, to me, is what always captivates me about artists, they gotta have their own. You got to be able to identify with their voice and their personality and style.

So things move forward. Next thing you know, I had enough money to put up to make things happen smoother. I think the best thing about it is, I was sitting in Oakland, but I only did deals in New York and L.A., and I only stayed in Oakland because nobody would mess with me. Nobody would fuck around and come in one of my studios, because they were usually in the worst part of the hood, which is definitely my energy. For the safety of it. I like being around people I feel comfortable with. People I can feed off the energy of. I mean all of my best developments as far as The Tony's came from, just being around the town. Get that energy hanging out, jamming with musicians.

So I think that trained me to look for certain energy, and with the girl group, the best thing I remember about them is I could tell they were sharp. They had been around some real pros. Before that, when I would work with artists, I only worked with ones that were over eighteen. That's what was unique about this. Totally different type of deal. Different type of way to approach it. It's more structure because you have to answer to the courts and people like that. You gotta make sure the young artists get— first and foremost (and Mathew was on this too), their education has gotta be on.

I have a big family so I'm used to a lot of noise. I'm used to a lot of personalities and stuff. So I think that kind of played a good part with me dealing with the group. That never was an issue. I think the one thing I was most surprised about after, when I look back, is that I was like, wow, that must've been something for the parents to trust me and leave their kids in Oakland for me to produce and nurture their act every day. I felt like, wow, you know, fuck love. Trust. People's trust is what's dope.

We moved the girls into Oakland. Into a six-bedroom house

in '95, '96. I had to furnish it and put everything in. Six bedrooms, over there by Lake Merritt. At that time, remember all those types of shows where all these artists are in a house and all that? *Real World* or something like that on MTV? This was the *Real World*!

LaTavia's mom was the parent that was there. She was the one going back and forth at that time. So it was the four girls, LaTavia's mom, and my production. She made sure everything was good at the house, made sure they were set up and had everything. One thing I thought about, the school thing is cool, but from what I learned, having a tutor that comes right to the house and gives you direct information is the key.

This meant me taking the budget that was cut to me by the label and using it not just in a productive business sense, but because if they were going to be a super group, they needed a lot of information. They had to be sharp. They were already dope as hell as far as I was concerned. The way they flowed together, the way they all got along, trusted each other, and built each other up. I thought that was really key.

You would have thought that they were kind of like sisters and cousins. So that works. I learned a lot because the tutor would come over to the house, sit there in the living room, and just give them directions, in Spanish and everything. At that time, I had a daughter, so it was really giving me a real clear path of how I needed to raise her, and that was very useful. I learned a lot from them, I have to say.

So they were getting good instruction then, and I think a lot of people think that was a missed thing because they went in so early. That's important to emphasize that I witnessed that they were still getting all the education that they needed. Even during those formative years.

I think what Mathew understood is that they needed to be exposed to people that could give them their information because that was crucial. That's another thing I learned from him. We had a difference at one point. We looked at things in different ways. I had to let him know later on in life, "Dude, I was nothing but a producer. I didn't know shit about all that stuff. So I was like a deer in the headlights when it came to that. So I was pretty much learning from you guys at the same time."

But we got into one thing when I was like, "Well, if Beyoncé is singing and everything, how come you just didn't bring me a solo artist."

He was like, "We'll worry about that later. They will be better when they get older to go out and go solo. I already have a strategy for that. For now that's a group, having them as a group is more practical."

I took that into my vault until this day. Today, I look into my vault.

Another thing he also showed me—I mean like this dude showed me so much marketing stuff—and he was not trying to show me, I was just paying attention: the simple thing of them covering classic songs. He was like, "I want you to do these tracks. I want you to cover this and that." So I learned a lot from that, and I've got to say that I went on to work with the Alicia's and Keisha Coles and all who came *after* that.... I had learned an awful lot by then from that experience right there.

Now this is just my side of it because I know there's like a whole lot that happened with them. But like I said, when they came to me they were so dope, I was like, "Why didn't this go?

These songs are dope!" I didn't understand, but I just went in and did me. I like music. I like songs, not tunes. So that's what I wanted to focus in on, and also, I wanted to focus in on exposing them to clubs and things around town where you are supported —the community. If the community digs you, that's your bottom baseline. If they don't dig you, you're nothing. That's the way I was feeling at that time.

I heard that the group didn't have the album recorded. There were songs that were demos that were cut by whoever the producer was before me. I thought the songs were nice, but I had to create a whole other catalog.

I knew Arne Frager; we used that studio where we recorded "Feels Good" and "Anniversary" and a ton of things. So I knew Arne Frager. But at that time, I really didn't even know that Arne Frager was the one that was working with them until later. Then I said, "Oh, no wonder you guys are so sharp! You've been around Arne, you've been around Gail, and all these other people!"

I always believed that group had something about them that was so special. Even if I wasn't part of the equation, this shit was going to come out. As long as you kept all the people that were full of bullshit out of the way. So I made sure that I kept bullshit out the way. That they had the resources to build. I think all of us were those people making sure that the girls were looked over properly so that they could maneuver through this.

They used to come to the studio and would be so dressed, they'd have on diamonds and stuff—always just young women. That was cool. I liked to see that they were stepping it up even though they were young. Dressed up, coming in with their little pump shoes and all that. But they were still young. So they would sit there with their pumps and I'll be like, "Hey, you know, you gotta cross your legs. Especially with skirts and all that." So yeah, especially we that had kids, were probably very protective.

I worked at a studio that was away from the 'hood so nobody could just drop by every now and then. I remember some rappers, pretty big names, would stop by the studio, picking up their information, or their masters or something. I remember one of them trapping Beyoncé in between the sound booth while coming out of the studio and I walked in and was like "Uh..."

He was trying to explain, "Oh man, she was about to walk in, I was just talking to her." Then I told him point blank, "Man, she's a kid, and she's here to do business." That's where you have to have those people that can keep you from that and sort it out, deal with it accordingly, and move forward.

I showed the girls a lot of things with style ... like the crazy bridges and things like that. Speaking of bridges... one in partic- ular was a song called "Bridges" on the first album. With us as the Tony's we always believed in taking songs and just going somewhere entirely different, production wise. That song "Bridges" was something that I took a vibe from an Al Green song. I remember us doing the song, and on that bridge, Beyoncé tore it up and just went somewhere way mysterious, and it sounded like some Abba or something like that! But when I listen to some of her stuff 'til this day, I could hear some of the influences. I'm like, "That's what I'm talkin' about! Build! Take it to the next!"

When I hear that, it makes me feel so, so good to know that I was able to give somebody information, and they took it and they enhanced it and they keep on enhancing. So that's one thing in particular. There was another time in particular when LeToya was in there on the mic, and she had to do this part. I know Beyoncé could have gone in there and just walked it out *boom, boom, boom*. But she was just standing behind that mic on the side, coaching and going over the song with LeToya. It must've been two hours on that one part, and I thought that was very big for a youngster to do that. Just to be the type that pulled you up, pulling you up. I just thought that was dope.

There were many situations like that. LaTavia, I remember the one song she ended up doing, when she finally got a chance to sing lead with a song called, "Sweet 16." I loved that song. I did the music for that when I was in high school. It was an acoustic thing I always played, and I never really finished it off but she came in and did it. I think I wrote the lyrics with Jody Whatley. I was working on that, and she didn't get a chance to use it, but the words were so sweet with those young ladies. Since it was called "Sweet 16," I was like, wow it was meant for you.

You couldn't help but see Beyoncé shine early on. At one point in time, it was all about image, and a whole lot of other things that made groups hit; you didn't have to be as dope. She was so dope. I used to call her Beulah every time she'd get on the mic. She would get mad at me. "Why you callin' me Beulah?" I would laugh and tell her, "Look, you just sound like a fifty-year-old woman on that mic, and you are thirteen, fourteen years old. It's amazing! You're like this little lady with this big voice." Like damn this little vocalist understands harmony. She understands where she's trying to go. She understands what lyrics not to use or what to use.

That right there is what really impressed me about the group. They were like a cold-ass basketball team. They understood how to have each other's backs, and one would pull the other one up. That's how I look at them. No, I didn't think I was producing the biggest group of the world. I just knew that they were so talented. I didn't think the world was ready for that because they sang too damn good.

When they came to me, they had interest at Sony already. But Mathew told me that it wasn't what he expected. Now I was used to doing deals at a whole other level. I had attorneys, and I had the right people, but the point is, I went straight to the person who brought me into the game—Sylvia Rhone. She showed me some real game. The first thing I did was send what I had done with the girls to Sylvia, who jumped right on the phone and called me right back.

"I really love what you did. I really liked that sound," she told me. That was the first time I'd heard that Sylvia knew about the group. I guess she didn't know that their name was Destiny's Child. I think I remember when Beyoncé said, "We got the new name for the group. Destiny!" and I ain't gonna lie, I didn't feel that at first. Why? Because I used to play behind a vocal group in Oakland called Destiny, and them dudes used to kill me! I didn't tell her that. I was like, "OK, all right. That's cool, that's cool." Then about two days later, she calls back, "We got it. Destiny's Child." I said. "Thank you!" I never told them about that.

Like I said, I didn't know all the work that, that Arne put in or anyone else. They all knew me, I guess they just never stepped to me and told me. But I just went in 100 percent and brought whatever I knew, like what we did with The Tony's. I brought the same type of engineers, etc., and that's how it worked. But when I got on the phone with Sylvia, she just let me know that, "Hey, I couldn't do this because of my allegiance to these people that know them."

I was like, "OK. But what does that have to do with me? I'm just saying, you don't think they're dope?"

She says, "I love them. Just make sure you take care of your business, right."

I said, "OK, I'm just a producer," to which she told me, "They're signed to your production. You got seven albums, a solo deal and all that."

Me? I ain't know what the fuck I had. I just had a dope attorney, that's all I knew about the business. I just wanted to produce. So when me and Mathew bumped heads—which I really thank God happened to this day—I learned there are no mistakes, only experiences. Take it and roll. I was in over my head.

One day, Mathew stepped to me on how he wanted things produced and said, "It's my way, or no way" or whatever.... Not knowing how he spoke or worked with a team, he said some words to me, and I got offended. I got Oakland in me, and then it went *that way*.

I ended up doing what's called a settlement. I'd settle with fewer albums, more control all on him, and less things that I had to be responsible for. Which is beautiful because that was really my opportunity to learn and grow.

So it ended up working out better in the end.

We learned from Arne too. In that studio over there, we recorded alongside Sly Stone and Rick James. It was like spirits coming out of there, so much was going on in that studio. They're telling me that Metallica used to be in one room. We met this dude at that time ... he was just coming up, named

Walter Afanasieff, and he was doing music for Whitney Houston. Narada Michael Walden used to be there.... So these are all the people that would always give us information. So we've been groomed by some really dope people and were just fortunate. Well, at least me at that time, I paid attention to a lot. You couldn't get this education at school. This was very hands-on. For the girls too. Just the simple fact that they knew how to maneuver the studio very well. So it made it easy for me to just throw out ideas or whatever.

A takeaway is loyalty and respect. We respected each other and the other producers, and being this OG in the studio, I respected them because I knew the information they had. It was very reciprocal, and that's what I get about the whole project, no matter how it ended. Besides, you know how they say "when one door closes, another one opens"? One door closed, but the whole damn gate opened! The Tony's were going into our last album together, and I didn't know that. It was just my brother was on this thing; he wanted to do solo.

When we were recording the last album, I went from one studio to another studio in Sacramento to record with them and I was working three or four studios at a time. I was doing Destiny's Child, I was doing Jody Whatley, and I was doing Karyn White. All these studio sessions and Tony, Toni, Tone's last album. At that time, they had so much stuff together. All I had to do was show up and make sure that things were signed off properly.

Their first song, "No, No, No." I remember hearing it. It was dope, and I remember Mathew saying, "Hey I'm looking at Wyclef doing the remix."

I didn't know Wyclef really personal, but I know him in

terms of his musicianship, and I could understand where he's coming from. So when I had signed off on something that he did the remix on, I was like, damn. I saw that song go from a slow knock to this whole other jam, and I just saw how people could work together and collab, not even being in the same room. Not even speaking to each other. When I hear the track and I hear what he's doing guitar-wise, he's speaking to me. I could hear him. He's never known that, but I'm sure he does understand because he knows that I'm a musician and a guitarist. So we speak that language.

5

DESTINY

MATHEW KNOWLES

Their first album was through a production deal of their own. In explaining the production deal: the artist is assigned to the production company, the production company is assigned to the record label. The artist is not directly signed to the label. They're signed to the production company, and the production company makes the album. So we had very little involvement other than "No, No, No" parts 1 & 2, "With Me" parts 1 & 2, and "Sail On" on the first album, because they were signed to Dwayne Wiggins and his production company.

Interestingly enough, that's the area where Beyoncé, especially, began to thrive. She's always had that extreme creative mind while in the studio in production, and as a songwriter coming up with the melodies, or giving out the harmonies to the girls. She's always been that person who did that from day one. She was more at home in that sort of environment.

Those skills became another part of her gift that I watched grow, and there's a difference between having a gift, being talented, and being skillful. Most people don't understand the differences between those. Beyoncé was given a gift that offered her extreme talent, and then she worked hard to be skillful; both are important. Some artists are skillful, and they work extremely hard on their skills to become talented. I would use that comparison to describe Beyoncé and Kelly. Kelly's extremely skillful, worked really hard to learn her craft, and that hard work led her to become talented; versus Beyoncé, who was given a gift, but worked extremely hard to be skillful with her talent.

Once the girls got signed and made the album, and the first single came out, that's when it really started because that's when the promotions began. There were demands from radio and television stations for the interviews, as well as the demand from magazines, and all over the world for photo shoots, the demand to put together a show and the first tour demands as an opening act. All of that required a lot of rehearsal time, and tons of practice, practice, practice, practice.

Being on the road then (being in two places required me to be away) had our family split because I would be with the girls, and Tina would be in Houston, running a million-dollar business.

Solange was just coming into her own gifts, and ultimately, became one of the dancers—but not yet. On the first album, she was in school but working on her craft.

I remember when Solange was in middle school, and I got a call one morning, around eight, from her principal who said, "Mr. Knowles, I really need you to come down to my office." The first thing, as a father, I asked was, "Is she okay?" He said, "Yes, she's fine, but there something we need to really deal with."

So I went, and the principal was there, along with the assistant principal and one of her teachers.

Solange had been given a homework assignment where she had to write a report regarding a poet that she personally enjoyed reading. Solange wrote her essay on the rapper Nas. Her teacher gave her an "F" on the report, saying Nas being a rapper disqualified him from being a poet. Solange adamantly disagreed. But what Solange did that made me so proud of her ingenuity and her business savvy was that she went and got all of the students that she could to sign a petition to fire the teacher.

I was sitting there with the principal once I found this out, and I told him, "I'm really proud of Solange. I thought that took a lot of courage because she's right, Nas is a poet."

The principal looked at me and said, "Well, Mr. Knowles, we'll change this grade."

I said, "No, the teacher needs to apologize."

That's one story I like to tell of Solange and her courageous spirit.

It was all very stressful in the beginning, being away. Looking back though, the travel became the easiest part as the group became uber successful, but it started as a real challenge for our family and put a strain on my marriage.

As we started that new path of success, I wasn't too worried financially. I made a six-figure income every year, and around, I would say 1986 and '87, we made the first million dollars at Headliners Hair Salon and made pretty much a million every year thereafter. So we were in a different financial position not to be worried about the success of Destiny's Child. As money would come in for Beyoncé, it was more of a platform to distribute her gift to the world.

However, even with that, there was a time, even as far back as when the group was Cliché and Somethin' Fresh, when there were strong challenges put on the family. Namely, once I had left corporate America, in the 1990s, actually. Then there was a strain in the air on finances, but I had Lil' O, who was doing well at MCA records. So there were dips and dives, even with money, but that was nothing compared to our emotional hurdles in adjusting along the way.

By around 1997/'98, and once the girls were getting signed to Columbia Records, it was like the girls went into overdrive. Their passion for the craft, their years of endurance and push, their teamwork … all came together, and everyone could see it. It was an unstoppable force (as if anybody much tried at that point) and a shining example of where they were headed. Beyoncé was extremely focused. Kelly was a loving team player. LeToya always made it fun as the jokester in a group. LaTavia, as the spokesperson, stayed energetic and outgoing as well. So they were having fun at, now fifteen and sixteen years old. Kelly was the oldest, then LeToya, and then Beyoncé, with LaTavia the youngest.

We're talking about only an eight-month age difference here, so they were teenagers. You know, I imagine as teenagers that was amazing, and exciting, that life. They were all over the place, on airplanes and staying in nice hotels, and they were getting notoriety. We were very blessed and fortunate in that we had a strategy for the first single, "No, No, No."—a unique one that the industry had never done before; and that was to put the remix that Wyclef Jean did on the album as Part 2. So, Part 1 was a ballad written by the Three Boyz From Newark, the three producers—Vincent Herbert, Rob Fusari, and Calvin Gaines.

Part 2 was up-tempo with Wyclef. Same song and lyrics but different tempos. We put those songs and videos out at the same time and it was almost 50/50 as to which song was played—50 percent played the ballad, and 50 percent played the up-tempo, which had never been done.

That strategy allowed the girls to come out the gate even with an up-tempo video and styling that Tina did—and it was extraordinary. Out of the gate—first single number-one on the Billboard charts and on into history.

Many fascinating backstories exist on that song and the whole era. For instance, Wyclef was in Houston, and the girls went to support him. He had his own solo album and was doing his promotional tour. I talked to him myself. "We need to do a remix. The girls would love for you to consider doing this while you're here in Houston. Maybe you can do it tomorrow." He was with it and said, "I like those girls; I'll do it."

I knew they were going to flip, so I locked it in.

"Well, what time is your flight?" He said, three o'clock. I said, "Well, can you be there at ten?" and of course he agreed. Be there at ten? Well, now with years of experience I know you're not going to get most rappers to be anywhere at 10:00 A.M.

Sure enough, the next day we were at the studio, having gotten there at 9:30 A.M. because that's how we were. Ten o'clock to us meant being thirty minutes early. Yet, to a lot of people in the music industry, 10:00 A.M., means noon. That's what ten o'clock meant to Wyclef, who was supposed to get there at ten because his flight was at three P.M., and he had to leave at 1:30 P.M. to make the flight. Beyoncé was really mad because she thought that he wasn't going to come at all. So when he finally got there, he was like, "Yeah, go on, Beyoncé, sing that song for me, let me hear it."

Since she was really angry, she just went into the lyrics and fired them off like rapid gunfire....Wyclef smiled, "Oh, I like that shit. I like this shit!" That became history as well. That whole fast-singing kind of style on the first album was born out of that moment.

By the way, here's an Instagram post I snagged, directed at me about this "No, No, No" song and video era. I think you'll find it paints yet another player's interesting perspective:

contentking07

@mrmathewknowles I tell a story your probably forgot lol; So, We're on the video set of "No, No, No" part #1 which I Directed along with D.Grant....Why? Bcuz you and Destiny's Child Told Them if I didn't Direct it there would be no video-bcuz not many know about the Lil O video story when the other label tried to get me to edit the girls out the video not only did I fight for the girls to stay in the video but I quit the edit. Now going back to No No No part #1. I'm in the trailer, and in comes the label folks flipping out bcuz you and the girls left the video set bcuz the label tried to make the girls wear wardrobe you(all) didn't like and your thing was (which I use to this day) That they didn't understand You Were Building a Global BRAND...So of course they sent me to go to the hotel to get you all to come back to the set which I Did. That's When I Learned from You buddy+ FIGHT FOR YOUR VISION NO MATTER WHAT. "DESTINY'S CHILD"

PLAYERS BEHIND THE SCENES CONTINUED TO EMERGE AS the group went through personnel and name changes. Having worked with us years before, with a background in media and the radio industry for over thirty years, Linda Ragland returned to the fold. She became general manager for Music World Entertainment and stayed through all the breakups and growth.

Linda Ragland
General Manager at Music World Entertainment

I MET MATHEW WHEN I WAS CONTRACTED BY A COMPANY TO handle their promotions venue negotiations and advertisements for their concerts.

Ironically, we booked Destiny's Child, Jay-Z, and Scarface in Mississippi. I say ironically because the concert never happened. The city received so many calls they grew fearful, so they put a parameter on ticket buyers, saying that you had to be eighteen to buy a ticket.

We eventually—the company I worked for—canceled the concert. That was back in 1996 or '97, and they weren't as comfortable as they are now with hip-hop and rap. They thought they might have some problems. This was Mississippi, but it was the same in New York, in Chicago, and it was in L.A., where they were just somewhat fearful. Obviously with the amount of calls that the venue was receiving, we were going to have a great turnout.

Destiny's Child was just beginning and were becoming household names. Jay-Z was already a household name and so was Scarface. I also say ironically because I believe sometimes in fate. They didn't meet then. Had they met back then maybe ... they might have hit it off. So maybe that was a good thing that it didn't happen.

In contracting with Destiny's Child, I first met Mathew Knowles. We're here in Houston, and he liked knowing that there was someone here who knew the industry. When I started working for Mathew, I was like, "Ah! I went to Tennessee State. You went to Fisk!" You know both of our schools are in Nashville, Tennessee. So that was a fun thing. I used to work booking a couple of acts when Mathew met me so I booked the girls for that Mississippi date, and then he knew I knew radio. He knew I had negotiated, so I think he thought, "OK, maybe I've found somebody here in Houston that would be good for this team."

Mathew asked me, after several dealings with him on a lot of different things, such as merchandising, to join in. I actually received the first merchandising contract with Destiny's Child. After we worked a little bit together, he asked if I would just contract exclusively with Music World, and that's how I came to work with them fulltime.

The girls in the group were Beyoncé, Kelly, LaTavia, and LeToya. It was the original four Destiny's Child. The first flavoring that this was going to be HUGE was a combination of things: of course the talent, but also the drive. It was something just to see the drive in these young ladies and the discipline, because there was a lot going on. You know they always say a star is born—actually a star is made. It took a lot of work on the girls' part and a lot of strategy on Mathew's part to make this group huge.

They ended up being the biggest girl group in the world because I have never seen such drive—I mean these girls were disciplined. "You've got to be here, we need to rehearse at this time"—they were there, and they were ready. They wanted to win. They wanted careers. That was my first hands-on work with a group like that. But just the thought of kids like these—I think they were maybe fourteen when I started with the company—I was thoroughly impressed. They wanted to win this fight. If it was: "OK, the limo is going to be ready at this time, you guys have got to be up," then they weren't draggin' them out of bed, they stayed ready.

It was a very close-knit group. It wasn't a large team when I was there. But the entertainment/media people called us about movie and TV deals, about people collaborating with them ... so the impression I'm sure that they got was that we were a huge company. I think a lot of that came from the fact that, in addition to being in the entertainment media side, I also worked at a bank, meaning I came from a corporate environment. Then you have Mathew, from Xerox. So it was a very corporate environment but also a nice family-friendly one. We wore multiple hats.

As a matter of fact, our first business cards had no titles on them. None of us. I don't even think Mathew's card had a title on it, and yet we functioned like a large organization. I looked forward to coming to work, I really did. It was like this was meant for me, and I say that because I've been called a workaholic. Honestly, if you weren't in that state of mind, you couldn't work at that office. You really couldn't. I say that to say we had a job to do, and everything mattered.

We may not have had the money, starting off, to send out and get a big media kit printed, but we had the talent inside of our office to do what we needed.

We got a call from a film company interested in the girls. It was just an inquiry, but they needed the media kit. We had one, but we didn't have one on the level that they needed it to be. So we jumped in, and I remember staying in that office till one A.M. and did not leave until I had what we felt was a professional-looking media kit on the level that would have been printed by a professional printer.

That was the work ethic, which starts from the top. Mathew was an incredible strategist so I was just glad to be a part of it. I don't like working for people that aren't—I hate that phrase but "in it to win it." Everyone knows that at MWE, everything matters, and everyone mattered. Everything mattered with Mathew, and that's how I've always been as well.

Because first of all, I knew that this group was going to be huge. I knew that. But in terms of the office. Let me tell you, if we were there working late, you could expect Tina would be comin' in with a big bowl of gumbo. It was very family-oriented. It was all hands on deck with just everything. Tina was there, and she did a lot of the costumes for the girls. It was costumes and hair because she was actually a professional stylist. So it was the image she was responsible for, and she did a great job.

It's so funny because sometimes she would leave her phone somewhere. So it's like, "I left my phone at the fabric store, if they call tell them I'm on my way back." But we were there whenever she needed us. Whatever Mathew needed. Whatever the girls needed. The girls were first and foremost. So, I enjoyed working there because these girls were nice, good girls from what I saw, and very disciplined. It's nothing like working for somebody that really appreciates what you're doing for them. I guess they were comfortable in knowing that we were working hard for them. As I said, we were a small organization, so we all did what our talents allowed us to do.

When I came in, the original four members of Destiny's Child, I believe, had just gotten signed to Columbia, and their first album had just been released. I worked a lot. I actually did a lot of correspondence for Mathew back and forth with Columbia. I'd started to work for them when he first moved into an office in Houston. I was working for him before Destiny's Child even had an office. Before Music World had an office. Well, Columbia provided a lot, but still, as a management company there are things that you will need that will fall outside of the realm of a label. Like getting inquiries about participation in movies.

That wasn't negotiated through Columbia. That was negotiated mainly with Mathew and the attorneys. Now there were always tough moments. Nothing's going to be smooth sailing. That doesn't exist in the entertainment industry. You know you're always going to have some challenges, and they were growing so fast. And so we were all working very hard during that time.

Again, I can only speak about what I witnessed while I was there. But I've never seen a group this young have so much interest. For instance, Sony Japan loved the group. Yet some of the challenges were in situations like when we were in Japan, and then a radio station wanted them here for a promotion that we're doing, and they had to be in New York the next day. Oh my God, I'm thinking. I'm holding up the fort because Mathew traveled also when they had promotional appearances statewide, in Japan, or wherever they were. I was back coordinating travel and everything else that was needed.

But the challenge was being strong. Honestly. The challenge was just being strong and doing what you had to do. When you're growing, you still don't have all of the funds to do everything that you want. So, Mathew and Tina sacrificed a lot to make sure that they had what they needed to look the way they looked, and to be where they needed to be. I'll say the same for myself. They would call me on weekends. I'll never forget when they were doing something for an R. Kelly CD. I think it was *Life*, the movie. R. Kelly was the producer for that soundtrack. I don't remember what city they were in, but wherever they were, there was a storm. A really bad one.

We had chartered a small plane, and these girls were willing to get on that plane in the storm. I got a call from R. Kelly's people saying, "No, no, we're good." When you're coming up, back then, and you had the R. Kelly's of the world, you didn't want to be in a position where we were scheduled to have a studio set and they didn't show up. So they were willing to do what they needed to do. But then thank God you have people that say, "No, don't. We can do this recording tomorrow." This shows, they were very driven. It took a lot. I'm telling you, Japan one day—New York or L.A. the next day. They had to travel in order to be as successful as they were. They made those dates, and the promotions, regardless.

"Our new album is out..." Not only would they go to the radio stations for the promotional tours, they also visited schools in practically every city. They were just committed. They weren't hard to work with. They weren't even all sixteen, so of course they had chaperones and tutors that traveled with them because the girls were of that age when they still had to receive their education.

Andretta Tillman was not managing when I came in. I believe she had passed away by the time I started working for the company. But I knew of her from the girls. They talked about her a lot. Sometimes you had challenges because, again, Mathew and Tina were parents of Beyoncé. You had three other girls, although, Kelly lived in the household with Mathew and Tina. So even though now we know today Beyoncé is a superstar, back then you had to manage the careers of four girls—a group—and try to balance as much as you could. Naturally you could see certain talent—like Beyoncé was the lead singer anyway. Always.

But I'll never forget going to a dance rehearsal. I was shocked. I went to the dance rehearsal, I had no idea that Beyoncé could dance. The way that she could move! I was blown away, having worked with them. They would come in the office, and we would have meetings on the regular with the girls. They understood the tour was coming up, what the expectations were, and all that. I guess I had just been in the office so much, I didn't even realize how talented Beyoncé was. Until I went to that rehearsal, and I was just blown away.

But let me say this: The girls—all four of them—were very talented. There was a five-year plan and a ten-year plan for development and their careers. We had meetings where we asked what their interests were. "Do you want to get into acting, are you interested in art?" You know, "What's your role?" There were a couple of them that had a great interest in acting. So that was the plan along the way, to get them to that point.

LaTavia, at the time, when they had interviews, was the designated spokesperson for the group. Keep in mind, they were all gifted. Beyoncé, I guess she was a superstar in the making. You had all the rumors that there may have been more attention put on Beyoncé. But I don't think that more attention is a reason why she's a superstar—she just is. Yet they were all dedicated. Beyoncé's talent shone in its own way, but they all had it. I don't think there was a situation where somebody in particular was pushed before the others. Beyoncé was the lead singer. Always the lead singer, is the lead singer.

If any of them had issues, they at least always had someone to talk to. Everyone listened and was there. Counseling actually was a standard part of their regime. This was before anything happened among them, there was always counseling provided. I think the counselor's name was Juanita Rasmus, through St. John's Church. With the history of girl groups having problems, Mathew just always tried to include some general counseling for them. As I said before, there were tutors that were always there. But it was a balance of good people around them to help at all times. It was an exceptional period.

Mathew was an extremely strong force. I didn't travel a lot with the group, only occasionally. Once, I remember the girls doing a sound check for a live performance, and the sound just wasn't right. Mathew—and they were young then, they weren't the headliners or anything—he would, I don't care who, where, or what, insist that they were going to get that sound right for Destiny's Child.

If Mathew had to, he would go and do it himself. He would cut it off right then in the midst of them doing sound check until they would get it right. That may sound simple, but it was very important. It really was. Sometimes some cameramen way back when the girls were like fourteen to fifteen, would have the tendency to try to angle the camera in a certain way and Mathew would stop it. He was on top of it, he really was.

Then I think, maybe, he appreciated having me there because I acted in the same manner, professionally, as he would. Because again, he traveled with them a lot while I was in the office. I actually remember Kelly's mom coming to the office one day, upset about something. I don't remember exactly what it was. When you have a child that's living with someone else, it must have been difficult. I had to really talk to her.

I just had to let her know that what was being done was in Kelly's best interest. I managed to track the Knowles' down. I think they were in London or whatever. I'm like, you've got to get on the phone because I think she (Kelly's mom) wanted to be more in the loop at that time. She wanted to be more included. I handled a lot of issues like that.

When the group got their first Soul Train Awards—that was huge. You don't get to take your trophy with you the night of. So when they shipped it out, they shipped Erykah Badu's trophy to us. It was like, "Yay, our trophy is here! Our trophy is here!" and then, got disappointed that it was Erykah's.

I remember that, as well as their very first Super Bowl appearance. It wasn't the grand halftime show; you know they have a series of events going on. We all went to Miami, and none of them wanted to go out or anything when they traveled. They went to work, and they went back to their hotel rooms. Well, Miami was a little different. I think Beyoncé fell in love with Miami when we were there for that Super Bowl ... she just evolved.

We'd look up, and we didn't know where Beyoncé was, and she had just gone to the beach by herself. We were like, "Oh my God, where is Beyoncé?" Then they wanted to go out that night. We were like, "What? I'm not believing this!" They never wanted that ... they always went to wherever it was they were going to perform, performed, mixed and mingled with all other artists or whatever it is, and then they went back to the room. Usually, it's get up, go to the next place early morning. But it was something about Miami. I saw just a huge change. I'm like *oh wow*.

Looking back, I can see it was always building up to be big. Before I even came on board with the company, I had the first merchandising contract with the group, and even today I have one of their first full-color shirts. Also the fan magazine—my company put together their first fan club and planned their tours. I remember our first tour was with Boyz II Men. We were so new. ... It's like, where do you get a tour bus from?

So when we pulled up for the first tour event, we were in the same bus line that Boyz II Men were in. We were ready. What we didn't know, we would do our homework to find out. So we found, and worked with, the same bus company for tours for a very long time, negotiating, trying to get the best price. "Deal with us, you know we got it, we may not have the money coming out of the gate right now to pay for the first week of the tour, but we'll have it when we get that first paycheck!"

I worked with the booking agencies as well. With Mathew, because I shared his work ethic, I knew what he wanted for the girls. I knew how he wanted his office to be run. If you've ever met him, you know he's a very smart guy, and he's very business-minded. I follow that model of how that office was to be operating. I was office manager at one time, and general manager for the group, but I also oversaw the activities that went on in the office because they traveled a lot.

Mathew was smart enough to know that in order to create the company that he wanted to have, he couldn't just travel and leave his office nonfunctioning. So we were there. Music World Entertainment was a real management company. I was an account executive, an advertising sales rep. Any hat I had to wear.

I don't remember exactly how I left the organization. We were going through some growing pains. We were growing so fast. I wore so many hats and loved every minute of it, but I was like, "There are some things that just gotta get done because we're going so fast."

When you have your eyes on the prize, and you have blinders on, you are moving forward, and you look up and it's like, oh my God, we have arrived. You've got to pinch pennies and do everything that you can do to get there, and it's like—we're there. I was there during that period like, "We gotta make some changes, we've got to do some things different." I had somebody to basically tell me—not Mathew, somebody else — "If you don't do this, Mathew's gonna do that. If you don't do this, Mathew's gonna do that."

So I actually wrote a letter to Mathew saying, "You know these things have gotta be changed." Little did I know, I should have gone to Mathew and just talked to him about what was on my mind. So needless to say, we parted ways.

I went back into radio.

Here's the thing, you can find talent everywhere. But talent will get you nowhere without discipline, a desire, and a passion for what you do—and a plan. Somebody's got to help get you there, somebody who, understands how to negotiate with a major label like Sony Columbia. You've got groups that made it, but they couldn't keep the deal. They didn't have somebody who could negotiate for them. Mathew was a negotiator, and he was a strategist. Because of that, he encouraged a great a team, and we were.

MATHEW KNOWLES

Speaking of teams…

The sound, the look, and the feel of the group that became Destiny's Child was made up of many parts and, behind them, many players. It would be one hell of a book to get every single participant ever involved to tell their version of the adventure. Thick and juicy, I bet it'd be. As it stands, this is my own recollection, alongside the memories of the available players we could gather in this time and space.

There were famous personalities who, while never being a part of the decision-making aspect of the group or on its creative team, had major influence on how the group grew. We would all cross paths with huge figures in the industry, even early on.

The first award that Destiny's Child received was from *Soul Train*. (The one Linda said they accidentally shipped that was Erykah Badu's. Still the girls were so tremendously excited to even be associated with the legendary brand). With the first album, they were able to get booked on *Soul Train* before the album was even out. There was a policy in place with Don Cornelius, a very strong guy, very principled. It was his way, or no way! The policy was that artists could not be on that show unless they had an album they were supporting. Well, we didn't have an album, we had a single.

So I'm there, seeing the girls finally (after watching it, dancing to it, and dreaming of it for so long) performing on *Soul Train*. They were ecstatic. I think back on those early days of the tremendous excitement they had and how they never lost that excitement.

At *Soul Train*, you do your rehearsal at 100 percent, and then you come back an hour or so later and start the actual show. Don Cornelius was checking me out. I'm controlling the rehearsal, I'm interfacing with the girls....Beyoncé is giving tremendous creative input, and the teamwork is there. Then Don comes over and he says, "You know, I'm taking a look at this, and these girls are going to be special. I can tell. I've been doing this a long time. Going to be really special. But I just want to know, how the hell did you get on my show?"

I asked, "What do you mean?"

"Like how the hell did you pull that off? They just told me you don't even have a damn album out," Don said.

"Well, what we did, I'll be honest with you, is because 'No, No, No' remix features Wyclef, we said it was Wyclef who was coming on the show and that he was featuring the girls," I explained truthfully.

He was like, "See, that's my shit. I like that shit." So me and Don, we built this friendship, and, fast forward, we actually worked in the same building in L.A. on Sunset Blvd when I was later at Sanctuary (which I'll cover later as Music World Entertainment itself expanded).

There, Don and I got to build a real relationship because I was out in L.A. a lot. We'd have lunch, and we really enjoyed the fellowship and friendship that we built from our industry introduction. He didn't do that with a lot of people, as he was a very private man. Don is one of many, who again, wasn't on the team but influenced it in some way to further us along or inspire us.

Other participants and group influencers I want to mention

here, who because of their roles, even while publicized, may not have had enough emphasis placed on just how impactful their positions in the group's development were. One pivotal person stayed beside me and witnessed the evolution of the talent alongside the child. When I look to the very beginning of one Destiny's Child member—Beyoncé, I see only the two of us watching the birth of the phenomena, long before the public got a glimpse.

Tina Celestine Ann Beyoncé knew what she wanted from an early age, so it's no surprise she could spot her own daughter's desires emerging, even as a child. Before she was out of her teens officially, Tina was in California, positioned as a makeup artist for Shiseido. She also loved to dance, and once choreographed for UAB in Birmingham, Alabama. Going out for a night of dancing brought out her attractive personality even more.

Whether doing hair and makeup or designing clothing ideas on the side, she kept busy doing what she loved. When she had Beyoncé, and then Solange, she became more of a homemaker. Because I was making good money in sales, there was a period where she could focus solely on motherhood—and to me, she was the best at it. I witnessed a devoted, hands-on, educating, and empowering mother who still managed to always keep her style sense glamourous.

Our home was practically an art gallery, with a lifelong collection of black artists' work and contemporary works in every corner. Like my own, Tina's sense of black pride has, from the time I met her until today, been strong and expressive—especially through her art collection. This pride and cultural knowledge greatly influenced her daughters and helped them shape their own artistic expressions of black culture.

Known for her generous personality and skills, Tina started to build a large but private clientele by doing hair. Yet by 1989-1990, with the girls moving toward the age of independence, she was anxious to explore more of her own ambitions. I wouldn't call it boredom so much as when a person has talent, it can hibernate for a while, but it ain't ever gonna retire for good. Tina's multi-talents extended into many areas, but she narrowed them down in the early '90s to hair styling and helping women look and feel good. So when I asked her what she wanted to do with that dream, she knew it was to open a salon.

I encouraged her to go to school to hone her skills even sharper, and then I watched her pursue her dream with much ambition. Eventually, she was more than ready to take it to the next level, and I put my support in and we opened Headliners salon. With oversized hair magazines that we published and the swift business the salon did in hair, Headliners became famous in Houston, and we made tremendous profits.

Once she opened the twelve-seat salon, she unwittingly created an *American Idol*-style platform for the patrons. There was time and space for impromptu performances by the girls, giving the "judges" a show with the price of their hairdo. In this way, we created a platform for the girls in the group to continuously sharpen their craft and learn to take critiques—even from ladies under hair dryers who were judging every move.

By the time Beyoncé started her venture into music, Tina was already deep into another of her talents—sewing and design. She'd come by it honestly. Her mother, Agnes Deréon, was a highly skilled and sought-after seamstress. Later, her mother's influence became the namesake for House of Deréon.

From Creole roots, Tina came into the world as the baby of

seven kids. Her hardworking parents did the best they could for such a large clan on 1950s wages—with her father being a long-shoreman and Agnes a seamstress.

Being with her mother and watching her gift at sewing, Tina learned everything possible about dressmaking from the start. By the time she was a stay-at-home mom, she could sit and sew anything ….from a ball gown to a prom dress in her own living room—with her daughters watching. Another of her early talents many don't know about was performance. She would double up on her skills when called for, like the time when she was part of a singing group in high school. She also designed their flashy Motown-inspired looks.

So music, art, and fashion were always at the root of her ambitions, and while they unfolded with the growth of Destiny's Child, they exploded once she found her own success—with House of Deréon in 2004, and later, her Miss Tina line in 2017. Yet, before there were big-label budgets and wardrobe teams, there was Miss Tina and her original designs—first for Beyoncé, and later for all the other members of the group. No event where her daughter appeared happened without Tina cultivating a look that eventually became a part of her acclaim.

Tina talks about her inspiration and her fashion's influence in her own book, *Destiny's Style: Bootylicious Fashion, Beauty and Lifestyle Secrets from Destiny's Child*. From dirt roads while growing up in Galveston, Texas, to becoming a prominent costume designer, to fashion mogul international, she pushed her own dreams through within the evolution of the group. Whether it was the matching or coordinated colors of the dresses, the Boy Scout uniforms, or camouflage shorts and hats for videos—the group's onstage and red carpet looks were shaped by Miss Tina—from the beginning.

Tina was needed. More and more, the demands of the group called on both parents in some way. Her input in imagery was stretched to the limit with so many appearances, shoots, videos, and tours. So one day, Tina had a meeting with the staff of Headliners Hair Salon. There was this Hispanic gentleman named Abel who had started with Headliners ten or more years before. He'd started at the very bottom, and didn't have a lot of talent, or skills, at first, but he did the things I said, and he honed his craft. He would be the first to arrive at the salon, be the last to leave after closing. He just did it the right way, working extremely hard, building trust in both Tina and the clients.

Seventeen years later…Tina had that meeting, and nobody knew why. On that day, she gave the entire hair salon to Able. She gave him everything—the name, the furnishings, the equipment, the clients, the phone numbers, and the staff. There wasn't a dry eye in the whole meeting.

It was at that point that Tina became involved fulltime with Destiny's Child from a creative and an imaging standpoint. A part of the group's success is the hard work and the creativity that Tina had and brought to the table.

By the time Destiny's Child began the Bootylicious tour phase, thanks to Tina's styles, their looks were signature and being imitated. Soon to be a fashion phenomenon, Tina's mogul status with her own lines eventually evolved into her branding a global enterprise.

Even after the group's retirement in 2005, she designed Beyoncé's gown for that year's Academy Awards. She also created the outfit Solange wore for the "Cranes in the Sky," video and another one for former President Barack Obama's White House–hosted farewell celebration.

By the time both of her daughters hit number-one on the Billboard 200 chart in the same year (2016)—a feat never done in the history of music by two sisters in the same year—Tina had cemented her place as a top-notch designer, and through those years, her position as mother stayed constant. You can listen to Beyoncé's *Lemonade* album and hear the inspiration, or hear from all the other members and team players and get this same understanding of Tina's impact. I know as a father and manager what it took to keep the balance and how much it took out. Only after many years, did I come to see the impact from a joyous one to a pain-in-the-ass, and understand what she was dealing with as well.

Looking back, it was not just Tina's role as mother, business partner, group stylist, and den mom, etc. that made her position so pivotal. It was her own talent and desire to keep her gifts alive that made her place them in the right position at the right time. It expanded into her brand while it shaped and colored another, making Destiny's Child stand out in their own fashion lane. Her efforts at it count as well because they were firm examples of persistence that motivated her daughters and adopted daughters to go at life with the same drive and consistency.

MATHEW KNOWLES

Here is where the business of the show began to be even more important, in seeing how relationships and projects, built and lost, would affect the girls. I could take any business dealing on the chin, I felt, but not these little kids who just wanted to perform. That is why I am most grateful for my background because it created my own industry foundation, from which many of my later strategies were drawn.

I'll illustrate it a bit to add color to my role as manager of the girls. I tell my own story more fully in my second book, *Racism from the Eyes of a Child*. But here are my personal CliffsNotes© that prepared me for the entrepreneurial engine we put behind Destiny's Child (in all of its many stages)....

I GREW UP IN A SMALL TOWN IN GADSDEN, ALABAMA, ON A dirt road with an outside bathroom. Ironically, Tina, grew up on a dirt road in Galveston, Texas. I never went to a black school until my junior year in college. So I was always the first in integrating and desegregating some place while growing up, and even throughout my career in corporate America—I was the first of "my kind."

I was fortunate to get a job at Xerox in 1978. That year, Xerox and IBM were the top-two companies to work for in America, especially for black folks. In fact, Xerox had been recognized as the number-one corporation for black people to work at because the company was progressive and proactive.

I was fortunate to sell copiers only for one year. During my ten years at Xerox, this was during my first year. I was a trainee in the engineering division of Xerox, which was an affluent one. That position led to me becoming a sales rep, selling copiers for a year, and I did extremely well, getting "Sales Rep of the Quarter" quarterly. Then I was fortunate to receive the best and highest honor available in sales and marketing, and that was to be in a medical division. The medical division was the number-one modality for breast cancer detection when I was working there in the '80s. Also at Xerox, I was president for three years of an organization called Minorities United in the Southern Region— MUSR. Our goal was to help minorities achieve an upward mobility path to management, with equal representation.

MUSR had around four hundred black sales and marketing reps, service support, administration, and managers. At MUSR, we covered an area from Texas all the way to North Carolina and everything in between. That was a big deal. In that role, I learned leadership skills and to how to develop leadership skills in others, how to lead and excel in high-level meetings, and about the role that blacks should play at Xerox and the opportunities that we should have there.

So, I had an opportunity to be involved with higher management before I went on to Phillips Medical Systems, where I was one of the first black reps to sell MRI and CT scanners in America. Then I went on to become one of the first blacks in a division of Johnson and Johnson, where I was a neurosurgical specialist, working with neurosurgeons in the operating room. So I had a different background, and that background has always helped me all of my life, and in all of my endeavors as an entrepreneur.

By the 1980s, when I was at the medical division, Tina and I opened Headliners Hair Salon. Anybody in Houston who's over forty, pretty much any woman there for certain, has gone to or heard of Headliners. We were that hair salon for seventeen years and did extremely well financially.

So my background was varied enough but still concentrated

on the two areas that would help us all maneuver through the music industry. I understood marketing. I understood selling. I understand looking at ideas from the 40,000-feet level point of view. Big strategic ideas, not small ones. I learned that people buy the individual first and then they buy what you're selling. There's no difference in music. I mean, the girls and their music had to sell themselves first.

I'd never gone into the music industry—I went into the branding, endorsement, and entertainment industry, which is different from just being in the music industry. My background gave me a greater strategy. For example, it allowed me to build a tremendous relationship with Walmart, L'Oréal, and other major companies. To this day I will always say the success of Destiny's Child, which ultimately became the success of Kelly, Michelle, and Beyoncé individually, was due to all the tremendous success we had at Walmart.

Columbia/Sony literally gave me the opportunity—and I certainly asked for it—to be the representative at Walmart for Destiny's Child. Unlike all the other artists who went through the sales division, I was a representative for the group. With all of Columbia and Sony film's support, I was the one who went to Bentonville over fifty times to sell in anything and everything we were doing with Destiny's Child and the members individually.

One last thing about corporate America. It gave me the skillset to be successful, I believe, in the music and entertainment industry. I worked with those multinational companies, especially with Phillips Medical, because the corporate office was in Eindhoven in the Netherlands, right outside of Amsterdam. Since I used to go and train there, I got to see the world. When I was at Xerox, in the president's clubs, I got to travel extensively … to Egypt, France, Greece, and Turkey, to name a few.

So it allowed me to see and know that the world market is much bigger than just the United States. And that was another way that we were different—our approach to reaching the planet-at-large.

The girls understood the processes: you go into the studio, you make an album, you select a single, shoot a video for that, then sales and marketing kick in from the record label, and the artist starts promotions. The promotions back then consisted of a lot of radio, because radio was a significant driver and a key to market reach and success. We're talking the late 1990s. It's different now. The industry is changing. Streaming is now the number-one thing that moves the needle in sales.

Our outreach took us all over the globe. When the girls would go, I certainly would go with them, pretty much all the time in the very beginning. Later on, in the mid-2000s, I could pull back because the team we had could fill in, and we were a great team. But in the beginning, the team was mainly myself, and the chaperones, because the girls were minors. Some days we would literally be in three cities in one day. We've done that at least four times. I've gone to Japan, Australia, London, Berlin, Paris, Mexico, Brazil, just overseeing one tour alone.

These jetlag jaunts became routine for the group, who worked extremely hard because they were so passionate. So focused. They didn't want a corner of the market to see them shine—they wanted the world. When passionate about your craft, it never feels quite like work, even when the schedule works you so hard. It's fun. You get to live what you're excited about. You get to see your dreams come true.

6

DESTINY INTO DESTINY'S CHILD

Kim Burse
A&R, Music Director

IN 1993, I BECAME PART OF A NEW PROGRAM THAT WAS
being implemented by Sony Music. It was basically putting A&R
representatives in the field, since prior to that you only really
knew A&R people as those who remained in the office. The
company extended its reach by having A&R people in the field
to help bring in new talent. I was hired by Sony to be the A&R
rep to handle the southeast and basically the rest of the country. I
was based in Atlanta, and they decided to keep me as the rep for
the whole country under R&B and rap music at that time. So I
could source and seek out talent for both Columbia and Epic.

A part of my regimen, and kind of how I got the job, was to
present my talent almost in a radio format, where I had a radio
DJ announce the artists and the songs that they were listening to.
I did this so it wouldn't simply be a tape they would put on and

play, and a picture they would look at that told a little bit of a story.

One of my claims to fame, Dionne Farris, was on the presentation that I turned into Sony, along with a couple of additional artists. Dionne ended up getting signed, and that was what led the company to hire me as well. So it was time for my second presentation because I made them at the beginning of each month, when I would turn in whatever talents I had sought out. For that particular month, as I was getting ready to do my next presentation, Teresa LaBarbera White, who was the rep in Texas, had come across a young girl group. At the time I believe their name was Somethin' Fresh. Teresa sent the demo to me because I was the person who would turn in the R&B and rap material to be considered.

That's one thing about which I do want to set this particular record straight: I never take away the status and the fact that Teresa was the one who found that group in this scenario. A lot of people sometimes get those lines blurred. I always let people know she was the one who saw and heard them first, and then she sent the tape to me. Then when I heard it, the thing that stuck out the most was the Michael Jackson song, "I Want to be Where You Are."

That was one of the songs on the tape Teresa sent to me. Now I know Preston Middleton was a part of that, though not at the time. He and I had known each other for years, but sometimes we'd speak and then we'd go for months, maybe a year or so without speaking to each other, so I hadn't been in contact with him for a little while.

I heard this tape, and I called Teresa and wanted to know who was singing the Michael Jackson song. The way this young girl was singing the song was so precise, because that song, vocally, for a child or a young person is hard. That was what was so great about Michael; he was hitting those particular octaves precisely, not wavering in pitch. Back then there wasn't anything like Auto-Tune so I wanted to know who was executing those notes just like Michael Jackson. In the chorus: "*I want to be where you are. Oh, ohhh*"—which is an octave, I wanted to know who was singing that because it was so precisely like Michael Jackson would do it.

To Teresa I said, "I really like this. So tell me the story about this." She was like, "Well, it's a group of girls. It's about..." I don't know if they were six at the time, or if it was the four, but I knew she was like, "It's a group of girls." She was like, "The girl singing that song. Her father is the manager."

So she's giving me kind of the 411 on the group's background, and she says, "They're really talented, they're young, and I like the songs they sing really well."

I said, "I would very much like to present them in my presentation to Sony next month. Is there a way you can get me a video?"

She said, "Yeah, I think I can probably go down and tape one for you."

This particular video is the infamous video that was shown on Behind the Music. That was very popular because Mathew is kind of scolding the girls for swimming the night before and being a little nasally.

That's one of the things I feel kind of always gets left out. I was the one who asked Teresa to get that video because I wanted to see for myself who was singing the Michael Jackson song, and so when she sent that videotape to me, I looked at it and realized, those girls really did have something special. I presented them just like I said I would. They were at the top of my tape presentation.

Not too long afterwards, the A&R staff, the field staff, was requested to go to New York and meet the vice presidents and presidents of the labels that we were pitching to. So we were all invited to New York City. Me, Teresa, and a couple of other guys were there as well. But it was the whole field staff of A&R people, having meetings with A&R executives, David Khan, and God rest her soul, Michelle Anthony ... all the upper echelon of Sony Music.

On this day, we also were able to do a presentation in person, presenting acts that we wanted Sony to look at, acts that we were excited about in the field. I was in the meeting, and I had my trusty dusty videotape from Teresa. A part of my presentation was to show the videotape of the girls. I showed it to David Khan, but I actually got reprimanded that day by my superior, Bobby Columbie. He felt I wasn't being a fair team player because I had a video, and the other members didn't have a video. We were only asked to present one group, but I ended up presenting probably about three. There were a couple I was extremely excited about, and it was hard for me, at that time in my spirit, to only show him one group.

So when I saw that I had his attention on one of the groups that I presented, I said, "If you don't mind, I'd love to show you this video."

He said, "Okay." So I put the video on of the girls, and as I was showing it to everyone, I said, "Listen to this! Listen to this girl sing right here," and I was pointing to Beyoncé at the time. I said, "You got to hear how she sings ... it's amazing for her age."

So she's singing the song and doing an awesome job. After I play it for a while, David looks at me says, "Okay, I get it." I took the tape out and I said, "Thank you for giving me this opportunity." Then he says, "Could you excuse me for a minute, please?"

When he steps out of the room, Bobby Colombie proceeds to reprimand me in front of the staff. "Kim, we were only supposed to present one group, you're presenting this man, like one group, and then another group, and then you want to talk about another group … that's not fair to your staff members, because everybody has come with just their one."

I openly apologized to everybody because I wasn't trying to be vindictive. I was excited. I didn't know if I'd get another chance to be in front of this man. I knew I needed to show him the things that I was extremely excited about in order to give these groups a fighting chance to be considered to have a record deal.

So when David came back in, he wanted to apologize to everybody because he had a meeting he had to go to. So he wasn't even able to hear presentations from any of my other colleagues. They didn't get to do their presentations. Then I felt awful because I didn't know he was going to leave or anything like that. So after he stepped out of the room, he asked to see my boss, Bobby, for a second, and then I apologized again, without my boss in the room.

I said, "Guys, I'm really sorry. I didn't expect him to leave. I just was excited." I remember Teresa saying, "Kim, it's okay. You are excited about it, and you just went with it. It's something I'm sure all of us would have done, because we don't know when we're going to have this chance or opportunity to see these guys again." I was very grateful to her for being so understanding.

Then my boss came back in and said, "Kim, can I see you?" I was like, wow, I'm really in trouble. He said, "You guys, the rest of you guys can take a lunch, and let's meet back in the lobby in an hour." I was like, wow, I guess am I getting fired, or what's getting ready to happen?

So Bobby comes to me, and he says, "Kim, I know you didn't mean to do that on purpose. Actually, David Khan loves the girl group, and he wants to sign them. He wants to make an offer for you to come off of the regional staff and come be an A&R executive, strictly for Columbia Records."

I was like, *Whoa, okay.* He says, "So, can you come with me to his office to talk now?" So he starts asking me what's the story on this group? I very much want to sign this group, he says, and, "You are correct about this young girl who's singing, her voice is amazing."

I said, "Yeah. I really I love them. I think that it's really going to be something, but I got this group from Teresa."

So he tells me, "I'll have my assistant call whoever needs to be called. But I want to sign them."

So now I'm looking at like another group that I've brought to the label in addition to Dionne Farris, who was about to get a record deal. He does contact Mathew. But by the time he contacts Mathew, he learns that Mathew had done a deal with Darryl Simmons and Sylvia Rhone at Elektra.

We lost the girls, and life went on. I made the transition from Atlanta to New York, became an executive. I was on the A&R staff for Columbia, and almost two years went by, and then Mathew contacted me and Teresa again. In between that time, I remember going to see the girls at a showcase that Daryl

Simmons had put on for them in Atlanta. They had changed their name again and were called The Dolls.

I remember going to that showcase because I wanted to meet them in person and just see if I got the same feeling that I did when I saw them on the videotape. So when I went to see them in Atlanta, I found out I still felt the same way. But for me being able to see them in person with my own eyes this time, and not on a videotape, that was when I really knew. I saw the magic of the group, and I thought, Man, this group is really, really good. Just within myself, I said, Man, they've got to have the right songs. They've got to have the right everything. I just remember looking at their chemistry as a group, even kind of sizing them up as individuals. Knowing that Beyoncé had the IT factor. I knew it immediately once I saw it with my own eyes, but there was nothing I could do about it because they had signed this deal with Elektra.

So there was another executive that came down with me, who David Khan had sent with me. So he had more rank over me, and I was a newbie on staff. So he went with me to the showcase because he wanted to know if the group was something that we needed to fight for. And of course, I said yes.

But we had a meeting about it once we got back from New York, and David just didn't know if he wanted to have anything like a true bidding war to try to get the girls from Elektra.

So we just kind of just let it go, and life went on. Then two years later, when Mathew contacted me and Teresa again, he sent new pictures and some songs that were kind of like free and clear. We wanted to use songs that Elektra didn't necessarily own. One was a song called "Second Nature," and there were some other things that they had done that were really cool. I remember calling Teresa and asking if she had been updated, and she said, yeah. "How do you feel about it?" she asked. I said, I still loved it. They still looked and sounded great.

I said, "You know, I never had the experience of pitching a group twice. But I'm definitely willing to do it again." Then she asked me if I wanted to have a showcase. I agreed, let's do that.

I remember two years earlier, when I saw the group at the showcase in Atlanta, all I needed was to see them in person and I got it. So Teresa set up a second showcase in Houston. She extended the invitations, even to the subsidiary labels under Columbia. There was a guy there that had come from the Work label, that at the time had Jennifer Lopez, and I knew that they had some things that were popping off.

Teresa invited Randy Jackson, who was A&R. He came down, and then at that time, the head of black music, Michael Malden, who is Jermaine Dupri's father. I can't remember if he came then or not, but I'll tell you about his involvement in a few. But I remember going down to the showcase.

The girls were great. They had grown and matured in the past two years to become even better performers than when I had first seen them in Atlanta. I was even more excited because they were developing into true stage performers. They still had great chem-istry together. The songs were still really cool. I remember saying to Randy Jackson, "Randy, we gotta get these girls."

He was more like, yeah, but the parents are involved. He had just had a situation where he had a girl group, and it had a lot of parents involved and things didn't go too well.

I said, "I understand that, Randy. But the thing is, is that Beyoncé is a star. You even told me some years ago that if you ever come upon a group, and the group has a star, sign the group. You told me that." He was like, "Yeah, yeah, I just don't know about it, with all the different parents involved."

Now, Randy was a colleague; he wasn't necessarily over me. That was just his opinion. So I stayed on the fact that we gotta get these girls to come to Columbia. I remember telling Randy at that time, "If you don't understand, they're going to make a doll out of that girl. I know this. I see this down the line that this is what it'll be."

He agreed, Beyoncé was definitely star quality, but he just didn't know. Teresa always felt the same way I did. She always felt like Beyoncé was a star and that the group as a whole was great. They were going to be something, she felt.

Teresa didn't mind sharing or delegating the responsibility with me. She was like, "Hey, if you love it, and you know that you want to present it and fight for it, then go for it. I'm behind you." She always made me feel like that. I've never had any animosity or anything negative from her whatsoever. So I remember going back to the office, and I learned that Michael Malden had written a letter to me and Teresa, saying that he had formerly passed on them.

I just was bummed. I was like, how could he pass on this? That girl is blatantly a star within this group. How do you do that? Who does that? Then what signing power do we really have at the end of the day? I talked with Teresa about it, and she said she'd just received the letter too. She told me, "It's unfortunate. I hate that he can't see what we see. What can you do?"

At that time, politically and diplomatically, within a corporate structure, I get that response. You know, but then I called Randy, who was kinda like my big brother. I was telling him, you know, what Michael said, and he's like, yeah and he's the head of black music right now so you know Donnie Ienner is really listening to him. I complained that it was just not fair, and Randy says, "Well, Kim, if you really feel that way about it, then fight for it."

I said, "Yeah, I will." I didn't know what my strategy was going to be, but I just could not let it go. So we had a corporate meeting coming up in Boca Raton, and at this particular meeting, there were going to be some presentations as well.

Once I got there, one of the groups that was being presented was a girl group, but it was a girl group (Xscape) from Michael Malden. I was just like, oh, okay, now I understand. He has the group he wants to sign, but then he came and had a talk with me because he knew that he needed me—not necessarily my approval -- but for me to be in his corner on this group, to help push it through. I will be honest; if that group had been better than Destiny, I wouldn't have had a problem going along with it because I'm a team player ... in the sense of, if it's great, let's do it.

But I had never seen Michael's group until that day of the presentation and hadn't heard them sing. At that particular meeting there was Donnie Ienner, President of Columbia Records. It was the west coast A&R, east coast A&R, jazz A&R ... it was anybody that was an A&R person—rock, alternative, all the A&R people were in this room.

The group on the tape began to sing, and they just were not that good. They just weren't. Like clockwork when the group finished, Donnie asked me what did I think of the group. I'm trying to be diplomatic and not be disrespectful, and so I said, "Well, you know if we get them the right songs and we pull it together, it could be something."

Donnie raises up in his chair and says, "Kim, I'm not asking you that. My question is, what do you think about this group?"

I paused, and I said, "It's just okay."

Then nobody said nothing. And he kind of was quiet. He shook his head. And he says, "I feel the same way. It's just okay."

Then everybody starts saying, "Yeah, I felt like it was okay." It just turned into like a movie scene.

Then I said, "Sir, if you're looking for a girl group for this label, I really feel like you should consider Destiny because I'm just going to tell you now, if you don't sign that group, you'll be making one of the biggest mistakes of your life and that's how strongly I feel about it." That was my time to fight for the girls. So once I said that, Donnie didn't say anything, but okay, and then we went on to the next thing.

The next presentation was Teresa's. Teresa had brought in Erykah Badu.

I knew Erykah Badu was a star. I knew Teresa was going to present her. They brought Erykah Badu to the New York office for me to see because anything R&B that Teresa had, they always wanted me to look at. I very much cosigned for her to be a part of the presentation in Boca Raton, but when she was presented in Boca Raton, once again, Donnie asked, "What do you feel about this group?"

I didn't say anything. I pointed to Teresa. I said, "This is Teresa's presentation."

The reason why I didn't want to say anything about Erykah Badu is because I felt that if they didn't understand Dionne Farris at my label, they definitely weren't going to understand Erykah Badu. He wasn't going to get it, and that's exactly what

Donnie felt. He said, "I see what it is, and she's talented, but forgive me I just don't get it."

When Donnie Ienner said that, I didn't say anything else about Badu, because in my own opinion, she needed to go where she went because that's where they understood her. That's why we all know Erykah Badu as a household name at this point right now.

I don't know who and what she would have been if she had been at Columbia, but I just felt like the people on staff at Columbia at that time definitely wouldn't have known what to do with Erykah Badu. Columbia had Alicia Keys at one point, and they didn't know what to do with her, you know.

So it's one of those classic things of "you choose your battles."

At the time, I wanted to fight for Destiny's Child, which was just called Destiny then. I just wanted to fight for Destiny. So after that meeting, Michael didn't say too much more to me after that, because I had gone against him and his group in front of the president of the company.

When we all got home, I later found out that Teresa wrote a note to Donnie, expressing how she felt it was unfair that he got to see that group but didn't get a chance to see Destiny. So he allowed them to come to New York to be presented to the company so that we could make a final decision.

So when Mathew called me saying, "Hey, we're going to come up, they want the girls to come and sing for Donnie and the staff," I thought, this is wonderful. Now everybody will see what I've been trying to get them to see. So when they got there, I asked Mathew, so where's Teresa? He says, I don't know. He says they just brought us.

Now you have to think about company politics. Okay, I fought for them in the Boca Raton meeting. So now I have to be the one to present them to the company in New York. So if this group doesn't do anything, who does that light shine on? Me, because I'm the one presenting them.

But I had no doubt in my mind about those girls at all. We met everybody on the twenty-fourth floor in the A&R lounge, and I had the girls go in. I told them, "Okay, I'm going to introduce you girls, and I'm gonna press play, and then you girls go for it." I remember Jerry Blair, who was over radio promotions there, and Yvette Noel Shure, who was in the Sony Urban division as the publicist, and who is still with Beyoncé to this day. A couple of more staff members from the New York office were all crowded in there.

I said, "I'm very glad for you ladies and gentlemen to be here today. I'm very excited to present to you this group. I feel like this group is amazing, and they're going to be stars. So with no further ado, please welcome from Houston, Destiny..."

I pressed play, and they started singing and working the room like they'd been taught how to do, and when they finished, everybody was like, Kim why did you need us to see this group? It's a no-brainer. I remember Jerry Blair saying, are you sending that to me? Now I need to get that on radio. I just remember telling everybody look, go to your office, bombard Donnie's office and tell them you saw the group and to sign them now.

Everybody was like—done! Great job, Kim. Wonderful. So they go back to their offices. And I'm assuming they all call because the next thing I know is the contract got presented.

Mathew told me that they were signing and then asks, "Do

you think they'll have a problem because we have a production deal in place with Dwayne Wiggins?"

And I was like, oh, man, "I told him you were going to be signing free and clear, Mathew."

He's like, "Yeah, but you know, Dwayne's extremely cooperative, whatever needs to be done, we'll work it all out."

At that time, I didn't even care what it was. I was just so glad Columbia was finally able to present them a contract that they were signing, and it was happening.

And you know all of that stuff got worked out. We started moving forward, making the record and preparing those stars for the world to see. The pattern of success started to take its course. It just got bigger and bigger. Eventually they did make dolls out of them.

Even when it was the four, with LaTavia and LeToya, I remember having a chance to be in Houston with them for a little while, and I went to church with them and took them out to dinner. I had a chance to bond with all of them on a little bit of an individual level. I even knew that LeToya was an actress before she even started acting. One of the ways that I knew this was because I remember watching the "Bugaboo" video, and there was a scene where they all had to act out in the boy's locker room, and she had the most acting ability. I said, "I knew this girl had acting skills." Now I'm sitting here watching her on *Greenleaf* every episode.

Yeah, you can say, Beyoncé is a superstar out of that group. Yes. But every single one of those girls, all of them, had their own type of IT factor. That's why I felt so passionately about them as a group and as individuals. Because what was amazing is to find a group of girls that in their own way had a certain type of IT factor because it's like, you'll look at groups like Dru Hill, and the only person with the IT factor is Cisco.

That was it. You don't really remember those other guys, but these girls all have individual types of IT factors that are going to make you remember them all distinctively as well as together. That's why I felt it was so important that whether I fought, Mathew fought, Miss Tina fought, Teresa fought, Preston fought, or whoever fought for them … they all had an inkling or understanding that if you gonna fight for anything, fight for this group because it was going to be worth it.

MATHEW KNOWLES

Teresa LaBarbera White is the one who found the girls as far back as when they were Girls Tyme. At that time, she had to sign them, but she wasn't a full A&R rep; she was what they called a talent scout. She would go around Texas looking for talent. She saw the girls when they were Girls Tyme, and after *Star Search*, and she wanted to sign them. We gave her company a tape, but they lost it.

So we signed with Daryl Simmons. Teresa was so disappointed because Colombia had wanted to sign the girls before Daryl did, but it was a timing thing, literally. I had given Teresa this tape, and she said that the Columbia label had lost it. Then I sent them a second tape. She sent it up to New York, and the mailroom lost it again. Then I kept calling. Then, a third time, she tells me that she needed *another* tape, and I sent it to her again. At this point, I'm thinking, "She's lying to me," so instead of signing with Columbia, we signed with Daryl Simmons.

But Teresa never gave up. She kept up with the girls when

they were The Dolls; she kept up when they were Cliché, and she kept up when they were Somethin' Fresh. That's when Columbia came back down to a showcase. Teresa has always been one of Destiny Child's biggest supporters.

Most of you have no idea of the internal fight that happens with a major record label, where you might have two hundred artists and you have to fight for budgets, for sales priority, international priority, for radio and video, and for marketing priority, just to name a few. Teresa was always there to fight the fight with me. Teresa was the A&R for every Destiny's Child record. Needless to say, she's done an incredible job, and even to this day she is still the A&R for Beyoncé's solo endeavors.

I remember when Teresa and I were desperately looking for a first single for the girls' first album. We met with producer, Vince Hubert, in a New York studio. He played a number of songs, none of which sounded like a first single. Then he said he had this one song that was written for his mother so he didn't want to sell it, which of course brought on even more curiosity to hear it. When he played it, Teresa and I instantly looked at each other; we both knew it was a hit. I said to Teresa, "I'm walking out of the damn room, I will be back in thirty minutes, I don't care what you have to do, but I want this damn song."

To this day I have no idea what happened, but Teresa got the song. Oh and by the way, the song was "No, No, No."

———

By the time the girls' career started cresting, and they were about ready to go on tour, I was beginning to manage multiple talents. I had a boy band on Columbia Records called

Sygnature. I had a female artist named Devin Vasquez, and I also had an urban boys' group called Jagged Edge. There was an opportunity for the girls to go on tour with John B.

It is hard to believe that Destiny's Child was the opening act for John B, but they were, because they had to grow. So, one of the challenges was: here you have some sixteen-, seventeen-year-old ladies—young ladies—on the tour bus with some twenty-two-, twenty-three-year-old grown men. That was a big mistake on my part.

I put them on the same tour bus because I managed both of them, and it would have saved both groups a significant amount of money not to have them on two buses rather than one. Then there would be times when they would stop and stay in hotels. One of the chaperons at that time (because the chaperones kind of switched out) wasn't the strongest of chaperones. I got a call one day from Kelly and Beyoncé, and it was basically, "We're really tired of this harassment by Jagged Edge." They were sick and tired of being harassed by two of the members of the boys' group.

That's when I had to make a decision. In Baton Rouge, Louisiana, I told those young men not to be on the bus anymore. And that's where this situation culminated into the split between the group that was slowly brewing.

I received a letter at my office, actually, it was faxed to me at first, and then sent certified from an attorney in Dallas. It said basically that on an interim basis, he was LaTavia and LeToya's manager and that they would be getting their own full-time manager. He stated that immediately, I was not to interface in a management capacity with them. I was really taken aback by this development. We were on the second album, *The Writing's on the*

Wall, at the very beginning of it, getting ready to launch. They had promotion requests, as well as requests for performances and tours.

I called the lawyer and I said, "Well sir, I just want to make sure that I understand this correctly ... it's impossible that a group can have effectively two managers because it's hard to make any decisions. I might want the girls to go here to do a performance, and the other person might want them to go somewhere else, or they might want them to wear this certain outfit and the other two girls want to wear a different one ... it just would never work." I said, "Sir, do you happen to have the album cover of *The Writing's on the Wall*?"

He was like, "You know, as a matter of fact, I have it on my desk."

I said, "This is the most important thing you need to know. You see the two ladies, Beyoncé and Kelly? They sang 90 percent of all the songs, so I think you're making a really bad choice here. I'll leave it at that."

If my timeline is correct, the girls were not even eighteen yet. Still young and naïve to business. Beyoncé didn't ultimately make the final decision on this idea, but she got the heat that she did. I made the decision! That heat she got should have been directed towards me, not towards her.

That's why she was so depressed for a period of time, because she had wanted to try to make it work. She didn't want to see the group break up and make changes. But they were all so young, kids still. The other thing people have to understand is that the label had to support this decision because ultimately the label is the final decision maker.

Donnie Ienner supported it. I called him and I said, "Donnie, this is what might happen…"

His response to me was, "Mathew, I don't give a shit about the other girls. As long as Beyoncé and Kelly are still in the group, we're fine. You go out, and you get two new members, three, or one—it's your decision."

This is the first time people are hearing what really happened.

What helped my decision, was what had happened a year before when the ladies were performing at Newport Beach, Virginia. The girl group Brownstone, signed to Michael Jackson, was performing also. We were in the dressing room, and Lisa Ellis, who was then at Columbia Records as a first-time radio promotions rep said, "Oh yeah, Brownstone just lost two members of their group."

This I had to see. The two remaining members, who were the lead singers, performed their hit songs, and the audience of ten thousand went wild. I locked that away in my memory, not knowing Beyoncé and Kelly would do the same thing for WGCI Chicago for their Christmas bash, with the exact same response —no one really cared.

Again, Beyoncé got blamed for all of this. Blame me, to add to what I just said. Then use common sense… No record label is going to, after Destiny's Child brought in millions upon millions of dollars and record sales, let a seventeen-year-old make a billion-dollar decision? Hell no. As much as we love Beyoncé, she didn't have the power to make a decision like that. People need to get that out of their heads … that any kids at twelve, thirteen, fourteen, or seventeen years old can make business decisions. Not just with Destiny's Child but in all of the industry. TLC were kids, Usher Raymond was a kid, Justin Timberlake and

NSYNC and Britney Spears were kids, and they weren't making decisions until they became grownups.

That's why they can blame me. The industry doesn't let kids make business decisions. Period. They can give input, which is usually through their manager or attorney, but ultimately the final decision is the record label's.

Well, here's some irony.... You know, the first album was when Dwayne Wiggins left and the girls were out of their production deal, which gave Beyoncé more flexibility and authority on the creative side. The irony of the second album, *The Writing's On The Wall,* said it all. Although ultimately LaTavia and LeToya were not in a group when the album came out, they didn't do a lot of the album's singing—probably I would say less than 15 to 20 percent total and, in fact, sang no leads on it... there was still an air of prophesy to the whole situation on that album, regarding them all.

The thing that has such irony was the introduction. The girls are imitating mafia leaders, and they're saying that *"as the four families, we must be United, we must be together... No more back-stabbing, no more lying."* And then there's a chime, and then Beyoncé says, "The writing is on the wall..." It's almost as if they had literally predicted this would happen in that introduction. It's almost scary. I mean, my hair stands up just thinking of how ironic that introduction is, based on what happened.

I DON'T SAY, IN THE END, THEY ALL BROKE UP AS THIS incarnation. Even as the final version of Destiny's Child—Beyoncé, Kelly, and Michelle; once they parted, I don't say they broke up. They retired. I want to use that word because they didn't break up. When you break up, that's because of drama. They strategically retired, and when you retire, you can always come out of retirement. So I want to help make that very, very clear, that the group has not broken up. They retired, but that team has been with them. One of the reasons is the support we got from Donnie Ienner. Donny Ienner is a fiery Italian, who even as Columbia's president was accessible to me, and we used to talk.

We both grew up poor. Donnie grew up in Boston, poor. I grew up in Gadsden, Alabama, also poor. Our parents were uneducated. My dad was a vegetable and fruit truck driver. His dad worked driving a truck collecting garbage. So Donnie and I used to say, if there were only two people, and I had to go down a dark alley, and at the end of the alley waited twelve people getting ready to kick my ass, who would the two people be that are walking on the other side of me?

For me, one would be Tina, and the other would be Donnie. He mentored me initially as I got into Columbia Records, and as he began to trust me, and began to understand my strategies because they were so different from what they were used to, he began to give me the reins that I wanted.

I had the ability to use the Sony machine and the Columbia Records machine, with all the resources that I needed to be successful. I owe all that to Donnie Ienner. He loved the girls. He wanted to see them succeed. He and Tommy Mottola, because Tommy Mottola was there in the beginning, and they both showed tremendous support. Tommy used to caution me all the time that he hoped Beyoncé never changed, and would remain the sweet girl she was, and not do what Mariah Carey did.

Mariah got into that hip-hop world and jeopardized her career and suffered.

Interestingly, my friend Don Cornelius used to say, "The dick rules since the beginning of the music industry. When female artists fall in love, they then let the men they fall in love with control their career." I can only say, with the fifty-plus female artists I have either managed or had on my record label, he was certainly 50 percent correct. It's sad to see.

While I was getting my executive chops, the girls were learning to nurture their other skills in music, like songwriting and production. I firmly believe that you have to develop a God-given talent, and I talked to them about being gifted and working hard.

I think you have to grow into being a songwriter. That's not something you just wake up one day and say, Hey, you know what? I want to write all my songs. Now that has been the death of a lot of artists because they didn't have the skills yet to do that. Artists develop those skill sets by being in the studio. Beyoncé was a sponge and was going to soak up everything she saw.

On the first album, the girls only wrote on two songs. It was only on the second album that they began to, slightly, write, and not on every song. Then on a third album, they began to write more, and Beyoncé again took the lead because the studio is her realm. Then, towards the retirement of the group, they were writing half of the songs.

So that developed over time. They had been in production deals before and had been limited with their creative input. Also, they were young, let's not forget. At the end of the first album, I went to Dwayne Wiggins because then, I had more knowledge and more support from the label. I went to him and said, "Dwayne, we understand this better now. The girls want to get more involved in every aspect of their business as they're beginning to get older. I've always wanted them to be involved with it, but slowly, you can't just jump into this stuff."

I really thank Dwayne Wiggins for being the man he was to step aside and not hold the girls back because he could've put up a legal fight and made a big mess out of it. But he didn't do that. We gave him an override on a future album. We were fair, and everybody walked away feeling positive. He walked away feeling confident. Thank you for that, Dwayne.

To this day, Dwayne has always been a gentleman and a true artist. So once we got out of the production deal, the girls were signed directly to the label, not to a production company. Now that allowed them also to get more involved in writing their songs and being a part of that creative process.

7

DESTINY FULFILLED

WITH BIG SUCCESS CAME SWEEPING CHANGES, FOR TINA, for me, and especially for the group, who had yet another—not one, but two, group change moves to make in a short period. Change was now necessary, with the absence of LaTavia and LeToya, who exited right after the management ultimatum was struck, and not without a lot of tears shed, heartbreak, and legal mess.

Enter Farrah Franklin during a brief spell between 1999 and 2000. I mean brief. I would have to say there are a lot of inaccuracies in her versions of what went down, at least based on what several of us, and others, witnessed on another side. I looked at an interview recently and saw she wasn't truthful. Let me say, many of these people imploded because of themselves.

We went into an auditioning process, as we had a short window to find replacements. We were all over the country, sweeping.

It was mainly Tina and Beyoncé heading up the audition

process. We were out in L.A. and they were in Houston, and then we went to Atlanta and all over, trying to find the replacement because we had the videos coming up for the first single on the second album, *The Writing's on the Wall.* So we had to quickly find a replacement. We found Michelle.

Michelle was a background singer working with Monica. We grabbed her up, and then finally got her deal structured and done. Then Farrah, we found, fit, and there was a strategy to that because we didn't want the imaging of the group to change drastically. The imaging was perfect because Farrah was shorter.

LaTavia was shorter. Michelle was taller, and LeToya was taller. Michelle was of a darker skin tone, like LaTavia. LeToya was of a lighter tone, like Farrah. It all worked perfectly. So the imaging stayed consistent. They learned and adapted quickly, and the image stayed exactly the same overall.

Farrah, to me, had average singing ability. Michelle had above-average singing ability. I loved her distinct sound. But what Farrah didn't understand, Michelle learned and adapted quickly. They learned how hard it was to be a member of a group like Destiny's Child and how hard these girls worked every day, seven days a week. Farrah didn't know that would happen. What happened was, we were in, I think it was Lubbock, Texas. When the girls started out, they would share rooms; Kelly and Beyoncé shared rooms. Michelle and Farrah shared a room. They were in Lubbock, and I don't know why, but Michelle really wanted to talk to me.

Typically, we talked in a group kind of setting. But she said, "Look, I just need a moment. I just want to let you know that Farrah snuck out last night. When we came back to the hotel, she went out to a club, and then she came back in the morning."

I considered this and asked if Farrah had done that more than once. Michelle answered, "Yeah, I just didn't want to say anything."

I locked it in my brain, and I knew I would have to use that. I started really paying more attention to what was going on, and began structuring the rooms differently. The girls had a promotion event in Seattle, Washington, with one of the biggest top radio stations in the country. Farrah did not show up, and we didn't have any advance warning.

Now I've heard her say she was sick, and she was dehydrated. Well, we never knew that. What we knew was, no Farrah in Seattle. Where's Farrah? It was the first time ever that one of the members didn't show up for a performance. I called her, with no response, then Beyoncé, Kelly, and Michelle also called. At first they got no response, no reply. Then finally we talked.

Our next leg of the tour was coming up. We were leaving Seattle and going to go to L.A. and then on to Australia, and that's a long flight. Farrah said she was sick and that she wasn't going to go to Australia because she quit. So she quit. The reason she gave was she didn't realize touring was this hard. It was just so much work.

WHEN DID THE FINAL INCARNATION TAKE PLACE, AND HOW? You see something that's changing, you feel something is changing. There were always dynamics, because earlier I discussed that when you sign a minor, you also sign their parents. I can understand that; I'm a parent. I always want the best for my child, so I'm not mad about that. But similar to Ashley, LeToya's mother felt as though her daughter should be the lead singer or have more of a role in singing lead.

I had a strategy for that, that in the beginning on that first album, you've only got a 10 percent chance or less that you're going to make a second album. So my philosophy was, we're going to go with our workhorse, we're gonna go with our Michael Jordan so that we can win this championship. Now next year we'll let some of the other players play more and have more involvement. But on this first album, we're going to go with the best ... what we feel is the best, and that's who's going to carry us. Beyoncé carried Destiny's Child on the first album, from her vocals and leadership to her studio environment, work ethics, and encouragement of the other members. I don't think that LaTavia's or LeToya's mothers quite understood that. I'm not sure even Kelly got that at first.

It was the strategy always, that on the second album, the other girls would get more involved with senior lead, and then on the third album, they'd have even more involvement, which is exactly what happened. It was a strategy that worked.

Anissa Gordon
Product Manager at Music World Entertainment

I THINK I STARTED... IT WAS ROUGHLY AROUND 1999. WHEN I got there, I was working with what's known now as Live Nation, but back then they were Pace Concerts. I was working there when a friend of mine told me about the company, Music World Entertainment. I sent my resume over, and they called me in for an interview. I met with the general manager, who was, at the time, Angela Phea, and then she called me back for an interview with Mr. Knowles. We talked for a very long time.

It was a very casual type of interview. I remember he was eating Tootsie Rolls or something like that. At that point, he was kind of just filling me in. There was a lot of drama going on. It was my understanding that the original two members, LaTavia and LeToya, had just left the group. At that point, they had just pulled in Michelle, and Farrah was pretty much on her way out. But for sure they had Michelle in the group.

I was brought in to run a marketing department, which he didn't have at the time. Back then, we were strictly a management company, so I was known as the product manager for Destiny's Child. My role was to be the liaison between Music World and Columbia Records. I worked very closely with Quincy Jackson, their label marketing product manager, and Yvette Noel Schure, their publicist—all the key players over at Columbia. We had daily interactions with each other, and that's kind of how it started.

Everything was so new. I definitely got the impression that for everyone, this was just a really new experience. People were still playing "No, No, No" on the radio at that point. It was all just brand new and people were trying to figure out what we were kind of doing here. When it came to Mr. Knowles, you definitely knew of his reputation as a no-nonsense type of guy. He didn't take any shit from people. I think he tried to groom us to be the same way because back then, in the music industry, these were considered pretty important people at Columbia Records. His biggest thing was to not let Columbia Records take advantage of the girls. My role was to be this sort of pit-bull kind of watchdog.

When I first came in, I definitely got the vibe that things were just not 100 percent settled. The dust hadn't settled yet. You could feel the energy. Everything was in transition, and it was kind of a little nervous energy. Like, was Michelle gonna work out at all? But you definitely knew that these girls were really, really talented. The work ethic that Beyoncé showed, I noticed that very early on; it was different. To me, it felt like she was very much like her father. She was a very driven young lady, to be so young. I didn't hear about her being out in the clubs or doing any of that stuff. She was focused on being the best singer and entertainer that she could be, and it showed. It definitely showed.

Back then, at that time, I was running the Music World marketing department, so to speak, and then there was a guy there that I shared an office with. He was running merchandise. There was someone there who did finance, and really that was it, if I can remember correctly. There also was a general manager. So it was a very, very small office, and we just felt like a family. I got involved during the second album. They were getting ready to release it and "Independent Women" was about to come out with just the three. This was going to be the first time that it was just the three ladies together. It was a huge success. They were very busy. They were touring with Christina Aguilera.

They began to get into things like acting and writing books (they released a couple of books). It was an exciting time. We traveled to New York frequently, working with the record label. The girls had all kinds of endorsement deals. It was a highly successful, well-oiled machine. It was fast times, very exciting. I worked on their second album. All the ladies started dabbling in solo projects, and then they came back together and did their final album. I left maybe a year after they released *Destiny Fulfilled,* so I was there through most of the experience.

Kelly and I had a really interesting and cool relationship. I ended up being her product manager after the *Destiny Fulfilled* album came out and she did a solo album. So she and I got to know each other fairly well. The vibe I always got, she was very close with the Knowles'. She was like a member of the family. That's the way I thought of her. She was a Knowles, and they treated her as such.

When I interviewed with Mathew, I clearly remember that he showed me a video and he was playing music, and I knew for sure that Beyoncé was very, very special. I'm not discounting the other girls, but she just stood out. I remember making a joke, that the angels must have been singing when she was conceived, and we kind of laughed about that. Even in my interview, I didn't know too much about the group. I just knew they were local girls from Houston, but it was very obvious that she was different. I hate to say it like this, but it was obvious she was the star of the group. Not saying that the other two were not stars, but it just felt different.

For me, I always got the impression that Kelly struggled with that. I always got the impression that there could have been some issues. I don't know if jealousy is the right word or not, understanding what her purpose was in this world, but I always kind of felt like there was a problem there because people singled out Beyoncé so incredibly much when they were together. I kind of saw that play out a little bit in her first solo project. Just her desire to want to be a big star here in America when really, her traction was in Europe and Australia. She didn't seem to appreciate that or want to maximize those opportunities because she wanted to have this big urban hit here in America.

There were issues on that front with Kelly. I did work Michelle's first gospel release. In fact, we did this huge promo for her album during the Essence Music Festival, and she actually got a number-one album out of that. We did this big mobile advertising promo for her, and a week later she was number-one on the gospel charts. I wouldn't say that I worked as closely with Michelle as I did with Kelly. I always felt like Michelle, who had her family in Chicago, was just a different vibe. It was newer, and you could kind of feel that. It was like a big family. We worked very closely with each other. There're still people from back then that I keep in touch with. There was Renee Lewis, who was Angela Phea's assistant, and she started out in finance. She was a really intricate part in pushing budgets through. Which was a big deal back then, getting Columbia to pay for appearances and tours and video shoots. Music World was coming out of pocket a lot.

So I worked very closely with Renee, and she actually ended up being my assistant for about a year or so. But we were like a big family. As things went along, that sense of family became a little diluted because Mathew was pulling in people from all over, and there were different personalities that were starting to come in later on when I was there, like people from New York. It felt more serious and industry-oriented towards the end, which was good. He definitely grew his company, and it became very legitimate. It was a legitimate record label and a legitimate artist management company. He did that through his very hard work.

Mathew is a Capricorn, and he is very driven. It always surprises me when people act like they don't understand where

Beyoncé got it from. In my opinion, she is so shrewd and sharp and driven, and it's not by mistake. She's exactly like her father. She's always thinking about new opportunities. "How can I market this? How will it look? What are the optics?" And that's exactly the way Mathew taught me to be and taught his children to be. His fingerprints are all over Beyoncé's career and even on Solange's. They grew up with a man who is a marketing genius, and it's the truth.

Listen, we've gone through periods where we didn't like each other very much. He's hard. He has reduced me to tears. I've been like, "I hate this motherfucker." We've been through those times. But, at the end of the day, you can never take that away from him, no matter if he comes off as abrasive or not, or if he curses you out. The delivery may sometimes be a little off. But he knew what he was doing, and even if he didn't know what he was doing, he learned very quickly and figured it out.

The culture at Music World... it was good stuff and bad stuff. Like I said, Mathew can be very, very tough. One of the things I remember is, he used to like to, occasionally, pit us against each other. I always got the feeling he did that to see who was the strongest, who would come out on top. But I know that he would sit back and watch us damn near "duke it out," and I think he would be like, "Okay, she won that." It had that kind of vibe.

It was tough. It was tough around there. You had to be very strong, you had to have very thick skin and not take it too personal, which is tough! That's tough for some people to do. It was the strong ones who remained standing, and in a way, I never could picture myself back with Mathew, but being back, it makes a lot of sense. It's like going full circle. At this point, I understand him so much better and I appreciate him so much more. There are things when you're younger and the ego is involved, and you don't want this man talking to you a certain way and everything. But I get him now, and I get his approach. He's mellowed out a bit, but he hasn't really changed. He's still the same. Of course, I've always been very proud that my name was attached to Destiny's Child and Mathew and Music World, but now I feel protective of it. It's weird. I feel like Mathew, for me personally, whether he realizes it or not, has an impact on people. For some reason, what he thought of me meant a lot.

To this day, I feel very protective of him. I don't like people talking shit about him. It's one of those things where I can talk about him, but you can't. So for me, there are few people that I work with now, and we all feel the same way about him. He means a lot to us. Is he perfect? No. He just wants to get stuff done, and I understand that. This man does not burn bridges. He fired me! He let me go, and yet here we are again. He's not that type of person who can't circle back to someone fifteen years later and say, "Hey, let's try this again," and I like that about him. That shows to me, a man who, number one, doesn't really hold grudges, and I like that about him. That's important. People come back into his life, and it's like old times, like you never left. Well, I think that was a team that was built since day one. Yvette Noel Shure was in publicity and is to this day. She is still Beyoncé's publicist.

Teresa was the A&R person who is credited with signing the girls to this day. She still works with Beyoncé and A&R. Quincy came a little later, not much later, but later, and was instrumental for years after the first album. She was the one that was in marketing and was the girls' marketing rep throughout their career. So we built this strong stability of a team, just like the young man Alan Floyd, who worked with Destiny's Child. Actually he was working in production when they were all on the tour. Now he's the tour manager, who to this day, works with Beyoncé.

So we built this strong stability out of a team and development. I can go on and on, from security to present stage managers, who are currently still on Beyoncé's team. Then their entertainment attorneys who were with them from day one and stayed with them up until the end, to their last album. There is also their business manager, who started with them day one and, to this day, is still their business manager. This was and is an incredible team. I'm proud to say that we helped put this team together that is made up of incredible people, and we watched all of them grow. Even then the talent of Beyoncé, Kelly, and Michelle, was absolutely awesome. Undeniably driven, undeniably talented. The work ethics from the ladies was absolutely always there. I will never forget.

Quincy Jackson
Product Manager at Columbia Records

(QUINCY JACKSON, WAS AN EMPLOYEE AT COLUMBIA RECORDS IN urban marketing. In fact, Quincy was the group's second marketing manager, or as we called them, product managers. A young lady named Stephanie Gale was their initial marketing manager when they signed the label. Quincy came in as an assistant to Stephanie Gale. This led us to Quincy inevitably being positioned as Destiny's Child urban marketing manager.)

I was working for two very senior marketing managers when I first started working for Music World and ended up becoming the marketing manager who had been assigned to Destiny's Child. I was Stephanie Gale's assistant. It was in the early stages; they hadn't been around long, and it was my first time on deck with Destiny's Child as an assistant to the marketing executive before their first single on Will Smith's, *Men In Black* soundtrack.

So I was working with the marketing executive when that happened, and during all the development and setup of their actual career at Columbia Records. Before that, I had started very young in a job at Def Jam, pretty much right out of college. I had only been working in the industry for approximately four months before I was hired at Columbia, and Destiny's Child started up quickly that year.

I had less than six months' experience when I was an assistant to the two marketing executives. I kind of was a powerhouse. I was very focused on learning everything, and applying the knowledge that I had, in terms of the marketing education I'd received while in college, as well as in my many internships.

I was part of the Inroads program at Sony. It's a program for summer internships, and you have to apply to be accepted. It's a minority school program that provides paid internships with Fortune 500 companies. When I started as the product manager with Colombia Records, it was literally the week that *Survivor* was placed in stores and was released. I will tell you, that's when I realized that although I had operated at such a high standard it was very important for me not to get comfortable. I'll say that I was moving very fast. I actually had just gotten another promotion. I literally started that first day, and I always carried a notepad and a pen everywhere I went, even going into the first meetings about Destiny's Child. I wrote every single detail down when I met with the marketing executive because I had to chronicle exactly what had been going on for that year. I had been with the ladies, and knew details, even down to individual preferences of each individual member of the group.

I remember the first time I met the girls; it was at a video shoot. I had met Mathew Knowles plenty of times, but now I was working with him in such close capacity, it was obviously going to be different. I remember meeting the ladies; they were very cordial, very sweet. But they were also very business-oriented. At that time (I'm not too much older than they are), I did not look at them as ladies who would potentially be my friends. I looked at them as businesswomen who needed to be respected. I think because I did not try to be too familiar with them, I stayed really focused.

Every time I had a meeting with them, and every time I saw them at a photo or video shoot or anywhere we had to do promotions—it was all business.

In terms of being an executive with the project, I'm probably one of the few people who joined at an executive level, who was not there in the beginning. I was not someone with whom the ladies had become comfortable and familiar with, like those they started off with and were in managerial positions. I will tell you, it's slow and steady that wins the race, and it took almost a year of operating in a business fashion before the ladies became more like family and more familiar with me.

We eventually built a personal bond, but even with that, the ladies would always joke with me—and I was always the long-standing joke—that "If Quincy says something, it has to be important." If I was warm and fuzzy, it wasn't commonplace.

And so when I had fuzzy, warm moments, they always laughed at me. I saw a lot of their warm and fuzzy moments more than they saw mine.

I enjoyed them all.

Obviously there was a lot going on. We had to survive the rest of the *Survivor* album. We had lots of promotions, lots of tours, and we had many strategic partnerships where I was part of the execution.

I spent thirteen years with them, so this grew into an extremely collaborative environment. Mathew Knowles, being the manager and executive producer, was a manager who pushed himself and pushed others, but in a way that allowed me to grow. Even with the ladies, things were the same. All of us grew around him. They had the same work ethic. If we achieved something great, we cheered, we were happy within, and we always pushed ourselves for excellence, which can be better, in terms of a competitive nature within ourselves, pushing ourselves to grow.

So although there were so many accolades that were achieved, there was always a sentiment of humility.

That was very important in terms of the collaboration, and especially when you have a manager who has garnered a lot of success, and a group that is winning awards and growing by the day—literally becoming one of the largest female groups in the world.

The girls always knew what they wanted. They are creative, and they had ideas for the group and a lot of insight as to what their fans wanted, and a lot of groundbreaking ideas of what they wanted to do, but they still allowed me as a team member to have input on larger decisions. It is important to have the respect of your clients, for them to listen to you and take some suggestions if they really haven't been understood.

Destiny's Child had a team mentality that many artists do not understand. Sometimes you go through ups and downs—something the group understood, I will even say, with *Destiny's Fulfilled*. Many of the concepts, the ladies had submitted. I also submitted ideas that I actually see reflected in the ladies and their solo projects. I knew them and how important their projects were, and what they represented and what it meant for each one of them. I'm very proud of how they stayed consistently the same, throughout and beyond their careers. By then I had experienced so many strategic partnerships.

Mathew has always allowed me to get involved, whereas usually record labels (because 360 deals didn't exist, and also because Destiny's Child was not part of a 360 deal) did not. Mathew allowed me to have input, and he allowed me to be involved as much as I wanted to be.

It was the first time I had been involved in a strategic partnership where we're really plugging in music, but it's a deal that rests on the management side. Normally, record labels don't get involved, yet Mathew always allowed me to be in the meetings with corporate partners and have a bird's-eye view of the negotiations and be able to submit ideas to him.

My time with Destiny's Child allowed me to be able to stretch my wings and be bigger than music marketing; it allowed me to learn and become successful at marketing. I'm learning about partnerships, about electronics, about networks, and within TV specials, even down to Barbie dolls, which allowed me to understand that when getting a book deal, having the ability to tie in promotions with a publishing house. That gave me a chance of a lifetime. It was definitely as if I had my whole tenure with them. It was more like having two or three roles as opposed to just being a marketing and a music marketing executive.

I wore many, many hats in terms of the final moments with Destiny's Child. I remember when we were on tour, and it was their final tour. I was on the road with them for many other dates, such as when they went to the Ronald McDonald Houses, going by to visit the children, so it was just such a bittersweet time.

The group knew it was their last album. Not everybody knew, as we had not announced it to the fans yet. But as the ladies went along on the tour, they were giving back to all these children across the U.S. on tour dates, and feeling that love until we got to the last tour date.

It was in Vancouver, and I remember they were getting ready to go on stage to announce that it was going to be the last time Destiny's Child would be together. They would have friendships moving forward, and they'd always remain sisters and always be close friends and family.

I remember them being in the dressing room and getting teary-eyed before they went out on stage, and it was very sad. It's the one time in my career I got choked up on a level that I had never really done before. After they announced that it was their last appearance together, they came off stage and we all were in the trailer. Another executive and I were in the trailer, talking to them and giving them gifts because it was the last sentiment. It was the last time they would be together formally like that or at least planning to be for a while. Beyoncé said some words to Michelle, and Kelly said some words. Then I started to talk, and it went back to the running joke that I really never get sentimental.

I always said, "I love ya'll" but I think the best gifts they ever gave me was respect. It was such a level of high respect, which is something that is so rare to obtain.

I got promoted six times. Starting from being an assistant, then being an assistant with Destiny's Child, until at the end when I resigned, in 2011. That was when Beyoncé was close to releasing her first self-titled solo album.

I was at Columbia Records when the ladies all transitioned into solo careers. This pressure was more than stepping into their first big promotion as a marketing executive with them.

I knew it was all on my watch, so to speak, in terms of what would happen to these ladies individually.

Will they have the success that they so deserve and are so talented to have? What can we do that's different? How can we push ourselves? That's not just from a perspective of executives, but that was in terms of Mathew and the ladies.

I went and studied, probably every day for an hour, after doing my normal role with Columbia Records and with Destiny's Child. I had to prepare for those solo careers. I would find myself putting together teams of photographers, and anyone who would work with the ladies who had not been used before. Finding new up-and-coming talent through new strategies, finding new ways of doing things.

What would be Beyoncé's story? Yes, she was the lead vocalist, but everybody was waiting to see if she was going to be able to transition into a huge solo megastar. She was going to commit to being a triple threat. I mean, now she's more than a triple threat, but she committed to being a dancer. She practiced and she studied. She looked at footage and made sure that she knew every exact technical aspect. Something that you don't see many artists do.

Funny story to tell… as we were preparing for the photo shoot for Beyoncé's first album, she had the title, *Dangerously in Love*, and of course it was a track from the album. We put together the photoshoot.

On the day of the shoot, Tina had pulled together these beautiful looks. Incredible looks!

It was the last thing we had shot, and we were at the end of the day, and Tina brought in this beautiful crystal blouse, but honestly it was a chain blouse with nothing under it. She held it up, and it was gorgeous. Tina held it, and I said, "I want to use this, I want to use this!"

We had run through the gamut of the clothes that we were going to shoot, and we looked at the photographer. He said, "Why don't we use your jeans," and literally that shot is Beyoncé wearing Marcus's crinkled jeans with a crystal top. We didn't know if that was going to be the cover.

I looked at Tina and gave her a look because a lot of times I would always give looks to her, and Tina would give looks to me —especially when we were excited about a shoot. When I got the shoot back, I pulled images, and Beyoncé picked all the images she liked. I sat there in the meeting, and I'm nervous because I really wanted this setup to be the shot and the album cover.

She was recording some music, and actually Jay Z was in there because it was early on in their relationship. I sat there, and I said, I really want this image to be. Well, first of all, I never spoke before she said her opinion because I didn't want to influence her in any direction.

She started pointing to another image but it was in the same setup, and so I was like, "Can I speak respectfully? I really love this image, and this is why: The orientation of your chin, how your waistline is curving, and the way your hair is blowing. It's the silhouette that just stopped me in my tracks."

I had stated my opinion, and I'm sitting there holding my breath when Jay Z goes—I like that one too.

Beyoncé looked at both of us, I guess because both of us said it was great, and she said, "Okay."

I talked about the collaborative environment. That's the one thing, no matter how much fame or success they garnered collectively or individually, that matters. The high level of humility that they've been able to keep is almost unheard of. To be able to still say, "I'm going to listen to everybody's ideas, we are going to collaborate."

For the rest of my life, as I look around the world and see teamwork and family, I don't just see hard work, I see all of the times when we had been up at two A.M. or worked weekends. It wasn't just artists telling me to go do something, or asking where is the marketing plan? Having this experience with Destiny's Child has given me an incredible and proud moment, just to say I played a role.

MATHEW KNOWLES

This incredible team has always been there. Frank Gaston had a reputation as a top choreographer. He had danced with Michael Jackson, and that's a big deal. But he had built a name for himself in the industry as one of the top choreographers. We wanted to have the best, and Beyoncé had done some research:

She had found out about Frank, so I went and we met. He agreed to come aboard as top choreographer. He has always worked exceptionally well with the girls because, as a choreographer, you get into more than just the dance movements.

You go deep into the core of the psyche of, "how does music make you feel, and how do you feel about yourself?" Because you're expressing yourself through movement, and know that is also a confidence builder because there is a lot of psychology in music. Frank always got that....

Frank Gaston
Choreographer

"En Vogue is someone I worked with prior to Destiny's Child. I did a few music videos like "My Lovin'" that won a few MTV Awards. The lady at Columbia Records who was in control of the video department for Destiny's Child knew of my work, and she asked me to come do the "No, No, No" video.

I'll never forget the day that I met Destiny's Child. As a matter of fact, when I used to live in the valley off of Ventura and Vine, I stayed at a place called Studio Colony. I booked a certain studio because I wanted to be close to the house, and I had done so many things there. So I go around to the studio the next day to meet this girl group, Destiny's Child. I had been sent a picture, and I had been sent the song because they wanted me to be prepared for rehearsal.

I'll never forget walking into that room and seeing those four girls. They were really young, fifteen or fourteen. I forget the age, but it was 1997, September 1997 to be exact. The thing that always stands out in my mind is Beyoncé, for some reason. How she looked at me like, "Who is this guy?"

I'll never forget what she had on. She had on a white terrycloth outfit. All the girls had on these really neat sport outfits that were popular at the time. It looked like somebody had just given them a bunch of brand-new sports stuff. I don't know if it was Nike or Reebok, but it was that kind of stuff.

I told them what I did. They trusted me, and we got right to work. I just remember after the day was over, after working with them, I remember Beyoncé a lot, and I'm not trying to put Beyoncé on a pedestal, but I've just got to say this—I left out of there that day telling all my friends that I had met the second coming of Michael Jackson. Everybody laughed at me. It was the weirdest thing.

My first job in L.A. as a dancer was with Michael Jackson, but Beyoncé just had this "IT" factor, where she just stayed very focused. It's kind of like she was in my ass to make sure that I stayed focused, and like, "There's no time to be getting on the phone, no time to be laughin', we're here to work because we're gonna make it."

The thing that always makes me upset with people is when they always say, "Well, Beyoncé was the start of that group." The thing that I want to go on record and say is that the group was that family's group. That's Family Mathew Knowles and Tina Knowles; they put that group together. Their daughter just happened to be a very talented young lady. It's very sad that LaTavia and LeToya are not in that group anymore. I would have never imagined that group would have broken up, that two would have left. Because they were just so incredible and loyal to each other.

I think they trusted me because I had covered En Vogue. They liked the fact that En Vogue wore high-heeled shoes or something. So I always remember that because they really wanted to know how to dance without having their knees bent. A lot of girls look like they are getting ready to go use the bathroom because they can't stand up straight in heels. Like you got to go pee or something, you know. So we did a few ballet technique things that day, just to show them how to "pull up," as we say. If you ever notice, a ballet dancer knows how to "pull up and squeeze" and really be tight, and they don't bend their knees. That's the worst thing to see someone do... bend their knees while they have on heels.

Because I gave them that technique right away, they really trusted me. Then I brought in four male dancers, and they were really excited about that because they all had their own partner. They were really like little girls—like, "Well I want the cute one!" I think, "Forget that, you should be looking at the one who's going to dance for you." But they really trusted me because I'm somebody who's been in this business a long time.

I don't look at what I do as being a church talent show. I don't look at it being a high school talent show. So they saw that I really was serious and it wasn't about brownnosing with them, and it wasn't about blowing smoke up their butts. It was about me being this coach, to make them be the best they could be. Then fifteen years later, the girls get off stage. Now probably Kelly, even probably LeToya because I know them still, and Michelle ... they go ask people, "What did we do, how did we do?"

People say, "Oh you did great!" but the girls will say, "We'll go ask Frank because he'll tell us the truth."

Basically, it's not that I ever said that they did badly, I tried to tell them the things that they could improve on, and that's kind of how that whole week of rehearsing for that video was like. I have videotape for that rehearsal, I don't know if Mathew knows that.

I watched it about a year ago, and it was just so weird to see how young they were, and how focused. I have to commend Mathew for really making them be focused because I work with a lot of acts today that are always on the phone. It's always somebody hanging out in the room, looking at you. We say, if you're not in here dancing, don't be in here, be outside because it messes up the energy. We want people in the room, working. That's something I taught them day one, and they kept that forever.

I have to say that it was just incredible. The girls did a great job. This is a funny thing, after the video was over—I don't know if you ever watched "No, No, No," right? There's some real grass there, and they have a bunch of sod. I asked the girls if I could have it. I had just bought a new house in 1997 so I put the sod in my jeep and took it home. I didn't realize I lived in the kind of neighborhood where I needed to put a sprinkler system in, and so the sod died. I always tell the girls that story, and they laugh. For a new group, they had a real budget. Today, people don't have real budgets like that.

So moving on from there, we started doing a lot of TV shows. I remember Magic Johnson ... I prepared them for a tour with Boyz II Men. Mathew would fly me to Houston. They had a shoestring budget, so I'd really work with them and they were really honest. I remember the girls saying, "Just work with us on a budget. You know we'll get you back in the end," and I wish people worked like that today. Because I truly knew, I put my investment in. Mathew trusted me, Mathew was like a brother to me. Just holding his hand through making sure that the girls worked hard.

I remember one time, one of the girls, I won't name the girl —when they were looking at the video screens and they looked heavy on the video screens, so I said, "Mathew, they need to go on a diet." He says, "Don't worry, they'll see that video screen, they'll go on a diet on their own." I'll never forget that, it made me laugh. Sure enough, they did go on diets.

I remember one time being at an urban network event, and all the girls were on the floor, dancing with some young boys. Beyoncé was sitting in the corner, bored like, "Well, I don't want to be here; I just like performing when you get on stage." I'll never forget that. Then I would say to the girls at the next day in rehearsal, "Now we're to have fun, but let's stay focused on our rehearsals, and let's not be bringing anybody who's going to distract you."

When boyfriends come into rehearsal, the girls act differently. They don't mean to act different, but they do. So, I would always lock the door, and I had this joke to say, "Somebody's trying to kill me so let's lock the door," and they would laugh. I worked with them for the next two years. I used to manage Tyrese, no one knows this. You know, they were so nice to me.

We did a Soul Train Awards, and if you go back and look at that *Soul Train* show, being that I managed Tyrese, you will see they let Tyrese be in their production number where they snatched his shirt off, and he stood there, blowing in the wind.

So Mathew was really good about sharing the light with other acts. You know, "sparkle brighter."

I remember we wanted Destiny's Child in the "My Way" video with Usher, but they had a commitment in Europe or something and they couldn't do it. Usher and I went over to their set and begged them, and asked if they could postpone their trip. So, Destiny's Child would have been the girl group in the "My Way" video with Usher, and that's because I was working with Usher. A lot of things that I did with the girls back then, I would always try to align them with somebody else. Mathew would always do that, too.

He did everything, you know. There's a joke in the industry, but I don't think it should be a joke, it should be right on. You know if you want to clear a song, Destiny's Child are the easiest songs to clear, because why not? If somebody wants to use "Bootylicious" or "No, No, No," why not? Why is everybody being a prima donna about not letting you use the song?

Now if it's something vulgar and stupid…. Yeah, don't let people use it. But that's one thing great about Destiny's Child, and even Beyoncé to this day, and even Kelly Rowland to this day. I don't work that close with LaTavia and LeToya anymore, but Michelle, Beyoncé, and Kelly definitely clear songs fairly quickly. I did a big Vegas show, and Beyoncé cleared her songs for my Vegas show immediately. I did this movie called *Leave It On the Floor,* and Destiny's Child cleared the songs and media. So that's it. I think that's a great thing, and my hat's off to Mathew for doing that kind of stuff.

People may say, "Oh that's greedy," but that's not greedy, that's just smart business to me. Let the world hear their song. I left Destiny's Child for a minute because I went to work with R.

Kelly, and I just got really dizzy. It's Michelle who got me back to Destiny's Child. Interestingly enough, Michelle was from Chicago, and she came to R. Kelly's show, the Tvtube.com tour, and she thought the show was incredible. She called Beyoncé and Kelly said we need to work with Frank. She knew I worked with them. They were getting ready to do a TRL tour, their first big-budget tour. Beyoncé remembered me from back in the day, but I had been away for like a year, I think. They brought me in, and the very next night, I flew to Houston.

The girls were sleeping, I'll never forget it. I remember the alligators in the backyard in a lake. They came downstairs, sleepy, as they didn't have that much time and I didn't have much time because I had to get back to my R. Kelly show. So we met all morning. We met all the way back to the Houston International Airport. And they told me what they wanted to do. And then I flew to somewhere in New York, and we put the show off for TRL. And after that, I was with the ladies for the next ten years and all the way to Beyoncé's career.

I just stopped doing Beyoncé for the Formation tour. I just stopped doing it because Kelly Rowland and I had done a TV show called *Chasing Destiny*. So they kind of pass me around now. I did Michelle. I did Kelly. Beyoncé of course. But ... Michelle is responsible for bringing me back to Destiny's Child. Then I worked with the three of them on a lot of stuff—Super Bowl stuff, NFL kickoff stuff, and the "Lose My Breath" video, probably their most expensive video—that budget was so stupid for no reason.

The director kind of overexaggerated things. But luckily Destiny's Child had that kind of budget. You should ask Mathew how much that budget was. But that video was a big-budget video, and the reason we had to go over budget was because while Beyoncé was in rehearsal, playing around during the rehearsal, she tried to do this split and she sprained her hamstring.

Mathew would always call that "Stupid Stuff." So we had to postpone for a week, but postponing for a week made the budget go up. The dancers had to stay around and Destiny's Child had to stay around, and I had a birthday dinner that weekend and they got me a big old pretty cake. They got me this Louboutin bag with the V's and L's on it. Brown. I saw it, and I'm not ungrateful, but I said, "I'm not going to carry this loud-ass bag."

Beyoncé said, "I told ya'll he wasn't going to like it," so they returned it for this really beautiful black Louboutin bag. Very conservative, and it had just one little "VL" on it. I still have it, I'm looking at it right now. Everybody I work with always laughed at my bags because, you know, I would probably come to rehearsal with a grocery bag with my stuff in it. So for the last twenty years, Beyoncé has always gotten me a bag.

So I have all kinds of these expensive bags. But this one, when Destiny's Child got me the one during "Lose My Breath," that's the one I cherish. I'll never forget how the dancers were like, "Wow, you're ungrateful." But the girls knew me to be honest and transparent, and they knew I wasn't being ungrateful. They just know that I'm very conservative. Beyoncé had told them, Frank is not going to carry that loud bag with all these V's and L's on it. So we just had some good times.

I remember my first trip in a private jet was with Destiny's Child; we went to the NFL playoff, and Beyoncé said to me upfront—the girls were up in the front and five male dancers were in the back, "We ain't never been on a private jet, and these dancers are on a private jet already!"

She wasn't ugly about it. She was just laughing about it, that they were on this private jet. They were very humble in the back, eating all the big old shrimp. But that was my first private jet ride too. What a great experience—the private jet. I'd never probably could afford it. But you know it was a really remarkable experience.

I did it again, later, when Beyoncé did "Crazy in Love." We went to *Saturday Night Live,* and I got to fly in a private jet. It was just me, her, and security, and everybody went to sleep. You know how you have all that booze and all that shrimp and all that sushi and all that food. I just was sitting there trying to eat as much as I could because it just felt that wonderful. I've had a wonderful time. They're like sisters to me. They are like cousins to me. They believed in me. They trusted me. That's why I was able to go on and do other things with them as solo acts.

MATHEW KNOWLES

Because of Destiny's Child, and Michelle Williams specifically, I started my first label. Because the strategy after *The Writing's on the Wall* was that they would do a solo album.

The good thing is Beyoncé, Michelle, and Kelly bought into my strategy. We did that in between *The Writing's on the Wall* and *Survivor.* We did it after *Survivor* and the next album. Now they all did their solo album. Now Kelly was an international pop star —especially in Australia and Europe, and so her first album was a pop album. Beyoncé, we know was a pop and R&B artist worldwide. But Michelle was gospel, and Columbia Records didn't have a gospel division.

I went to Donnie Ienner and said, "Look, Michelle wants to do a gospel record. I've researched that industry, and I'm not impressed. I can't afford for Michelle to fail because if she fails, then the brand of Destiny's Child fails as well, and we can't have that." He says, "You're absolutely right. What do we do?"

I answered, "I'm going to have to form a gospel record label." He says, "All right, then do it."

Columbia Records founded Music World Gospel and that's how it was born. That's how we got started. Prior to that, and afterwards, we had the Music World imprint, but this was truly a staff and record label. We named it Music World Gospel. I didn't have a joint venture with Columbia on Destiny Child's third album, but unfortunately, I cross-collateralized Music World's income because, unselfishly, I wanted Kelly and Michelle to be successful.

Columbia and Music World overspent millions of dollars. So whenever someone says I didn't do the best for Kelly and Michelle that is a bald-faced lie. In fact I lost about 1.5 million on their combined projects.

In 2002, and Destiny's Child would have been on the third album, was when Michelle launched her solo and I started the label. Then I sold Music World, the management company, to this London-based company called Sanctuary, who had the largest independent record label and independent management and merchandise company in the world. They bought Music World, and I became the president. We formed a division called Music World/Sanctuary London. We were a record label, and we were a management company, and not only was I the president of that division, I was number 10 in a company of about 750 employees, all based in London, the U.S.A., and Germany.

We had offices now in Houston, in Los Angeles, and in New York—and now I'm traveling all over the world. I built a staff that mirrored Columbia Records. We had forty-five employees just in Houston. We had our own product manager, our whole sales team, and we made sure that we never had to depend on Columbia Records solely, but that we were a team, and we added value by having the same team they had. With Sanctuary, under our record label, we brought on Earth Wind and Fire, The O' Jays, Chaka Khan, and Kool and the Gang. We brought Michelle's and Solange's first album over from Sony.

We had Ray J and Jon B. on the label. On the management side, I went out and bought five urban management companies. Troy Carter, Julius Erving II, Jeremey Geffen and Max Goose, Kendall Isaacs, Demmette Guidry and Nelly's manager Tony. From those managers, and after buying their companies, we now had Mary J. Blige, Eve, Floetry, D12, and Mary Mary as part of our urban management company. We also had from Music World management: Mario, Solange, Destiny's Child, Beyoncé, Kelly, and Michelle, as well as their individual solo careers.

We became the largest urban management company that was built. It did extremely well, but that took away a lot of my time from focusing on Destiny's Child, Solange, and their individual careers. It began to take away from me being a husband and a father. I think it's important that we talk more about their solo projects, albums, and the impact they had because the strategy was, that if each one of the girls built their solo careers, they were bringing back a larger audience to Destiny's Child because they were garnishing a large new audience. All of their solo albums debuted at number-one.

Then it often angers me—and Beyoncé is my daughter, but it sometimes angers me that the marketplace and the industry forget the individual successes of Kelly and Michelle. Kelly's first album had Nelly on the single, and it went number-one1 and the song won a Grammy. Kelly had a number-one album outside of America, but she was hardheaded. She didn't listen to what I had suggested to her, which was to become an international pop star and not worry about America. But folks got in her head and made her think that she should be a R&B artist, and they always tried to compare her to Beyoncé in saying, "All they do is help Beyoncé," so she got off the strategy. She didn't follow the game plan and tried to come up with her own game plan. Unfortunately, that hasn't been very successful. Not at all.

Michelle stayed on her game plan for the most part, but for some of the same reasons as Kelly, she did attempt, while on Music World Columbia, to make a dance pop album that didn't work. As I said earlier, I wanted all three of the ladies of Destiny's Child to have a successful music career and an entertainment career even after the group. I supported their visions even when I didn't agree.

I fault the media for that as well. I fault the individual fans for pitting Kelly, Michelle, and Beyoncé against each other. There's 7.5 billion people who live on this planet, only 325 million live in United States. Kelly was never supposed to be a U.S. artist. Kelly was the international artist. So while people in America are, say, all about Beyoncé, people in Australia are, saying all these things about Kelly. I am proud today that Kelly still has that fan base. We've always said, "Kelly would be the

Tina Turner of Europe. You can be the same as Sade, both in Europe and Australia. That could be you."

MEANWHILE, SOLANGE GOT HER OWN DEAL. SHE WAS A lead dancer with Destiny's Child. She co-wrote 50 percent of Kelly's first album and co-wrote a lot of those hit songs for Destiny's Child like, "Get Me Bodied," and I could go on. When Kelly broke her toe on the Christina Aguilera tour, Solange stepped up and played Kelly's role. Do you want to know how Kelly broke her toe? Well, Destiny's Child and Christina Aguilera were on tour together, playing in amphitheaters. Christina really had only a couple of hit songs at that time, but do I need to say any more? Christina's management team was super arrogant, with lots of ego (ego is the anesthesia that deadens the pain of stupidity). They wouldn't allow Destiny's Child to use her quick change booth, which was a 5x5 area draped with a black curtain next to the stage, so the ladies, who had more clothing changes than Christina, had to run full speed to the loading dock and be back in two minutes. You get the idea... that's how Solange filled in after Kelly's accident.

I worked very hard to get Solange the singing lead on the animated TV series, *The Proud Family*, with Destiny's Child singing the backup. I wanted Solange to experience Destiny's Child and be a part of them. Solange developed her gift of penmanship at a very early age. I always wanted Solange to be a member of Destiny's Child, but she never wanted it. I never was the parent or manager to force my kids to do something they didn't want to do. Solange always wanted to go solo, which is why she named her first album, *Solo Star*.

When LeToya and LaTavia left the group, instead of having to find two people, we thought, let Solange do it, that would've been the solution, but she didn't want to do that. So that was never forced upon her.

With the success of the solo albums, their growth became more apparent because they could begin to better understand and become more focused on understanding the business side of the industry. They still have a lot of growth to do, even now on the business side of it. It's hard for any artist to be the best in business and artistry because when you're truly giving 100 percent of your artistry, you don't have the time or brain-width for business. It takes a lot of strength to be the artist and be the boss of your own business too.

Beyoncé has told the story, and she's told it accurately. It was 1997, and there was an FM radio station in Houston, and on that DJ's morning show (where you know DJs are trying to bring their numbers up because that's the morning drive time and so you create drama—that's part of the gig), the DJ said, "Hey, who's going to be next to survive the next Destiny's Child?" Because at that time *Survivor* was the number-one TV show.

Beyoncé actually heard that and it angered her. She went and wrote the song called "Survivor." Most people don't even know: That's me chanting and humming on the song. They all contributed, and everybody was proud. They all had even of a more sense of pride since they all had their own number-one albums at that time. A lot of hard work, but they are making significant money, and they're getting older now.

They are not teenagers anymore. They're women. They lasted

through so much. I've said it once, I'm gonna say it again: There was never, ever a breakup. There was an award show where they announced that they were retiring. You've never heard any member of that group say that we "broke up." They retired … you don't get fired when you retire. You decide you want to leave, and you do. But the great thing about retirement is, you can always go back, just like Destiny's Child will one day. Hopefully we'll do that one last record—no! Not another record—I'm not so much hoping they'll do another record. I hope they do one more tour before they get older and before we don't want to see them once they have gotten older, when bodies change. We want to see Destiny's Child now and remember them like their destiny was fulfilled.

Destiny was fulfilled, and that was the title of the last studio album before the *Greatest Hits*. How prophetic that they named their last album, *Destiny Fulfilled*. On their last album they were really involved, and very excited and engaged, as if it was their first. You know when you've gotten that many number-ones, Grammys, tours… and are around each other almost 70 percent of the time, and you now have families and relationships; sometimes, lasting friendships are way more important. You just get tired a little bit and you say, "Hey, I don't want to work this hard. Or if I do, I'll just go out and do it on my own." So I think it was a combination of all of that.

Right in the middle of that process, Farrah was no longer in a group. It was just Michelle, Kelly, and Beyoncé. Beyoncé's solo career was really outpacing the other girls' and it always would outpace them. It's a natural transition with groups that has happened since the history of the music business. The Supremes —the person who outpaced the other ladies was Diana Ross.

When we look at NSYNC, the person who outpaced the others in a group was Justin Timberlake. Patti LaBelle of the Labelle's? Patti outpaced everybody! So I think it was a combination of a number of things like, "Look, now we all have financial freedom. We all have a collective, but now also a personal thing is happening." I think, at this point there were outside influences saying, "You know, girl, you gotta just do this by yourself."

Jennette Everett
Fan Club Manager & Creator of Beyhive

I'LL NEVER FORGET THE DAY I FOUND OUT ABOUT THIS JOB: Friday, July 27, 2001. I got a call from a college acquaintance, telling me that they had a lead on a job for me to work with Destiny's Child. I thought he was full of it. Sure enough, I got a call for an interview the following Monday, and by Wednesday after three interviews I was offered the job. It was a whirlwind experience because I was told I had to be in NYC on Saturday, August 11 to join up with Destiny's Child on the TRL Tour, which was already in progress. I remember flying into NYC and thinking I was dreaming…that there was no way that I was going on the road with Destiny's Child. I enjoyed their music and was certainly a fan, but not like the fans I would soon meet, that's for sure. I spent the next six weeks on tour, running the fan club booth with another employee, Jonathan Cooks.

We would set up this interactive booth at every show where fans could play trivia games on touchscreen computers and win prizes including fan club memberships. The TRL Tour was cut short by the events of September 11, 2001. We were supposed to be heading into Canada on the morning of September 11, 2001 but instead, we ended up camped out in motels in Everett, Washington, for four or five days while chaos ensued.

The Canadian border was closed, and air travel was at a standstill, so management divided us up by home locations and used the tour buses to get us home. It was a crazy time. I spent six weeks on the road with them, and yet I never met the ladies of Destiny's Child. I would see them in passing backstage, but we were never introduced.

I went back to Houston and worked out of the Music World Entertainment offices at 9898 Bissonnet. My daily job consisted of opening fan mail, messaging fans on the message boards, answering emails, and packaging fan club memberships that were sold online. I had an assistant named Deniro Basden, and we worked well together.

In the fall of 2001, the anthrax terror attacks were happening, so to open fan mail in the office we would wear gloves and masks—it was quite the sight to be seen! We had one scare, but it turned out to be just some glitter that a fan had included in their envelope!

My introduction to Destiny's Child would come the following summer in 2002 when we were in Europe in May/June 2002 doing the tour that was supposed to happen immediately following the TRL tour in fall 2001, but it was rescheduled for summer 2002. I mentioned to Alan Floyd, who at the time was working as their photographer (but later became their tour manager and continues to do that for Beyoncé to this day), that we had never met, and he said we have to fix that.

So he introduced me the next night, after the fans had finished their Meet & Greet. They said, "You're Jennette? Our fans keep telling us about you, and we were like 'who's Jennette?' You're doing a great job—keep it up!"

I had spent the last year building up their fan base online through the Destiny's Child Message Boards and had built trust with the fans as the moderator and Fan Club Manager, so it only made sense that the fans would mention me by name.

It was on this tour in summer of 2002 that we met the five fans that would later become known to Destiny's Child and me as the Fab Five: Richard, Jody, Jamie, Laura, and Tazmin. Five fans that met on the Destiny's Child fan club message boards and started going to multiple shows together. They were beyond dedicated as fans, and so much fun. Meeting the Destiny's Child fans was the best part of my job. Some amazing people, including the Fab Five who have become lifelong friends of mine along the way.

I celebrated my twenty-fourth birthday on tour in June 2002. The catering crew made me a raspberry cheesecake that was out of this world, and during the Meet & Greet that night the ladies of Destiny's Child sang me happy birthday. By this point I was seeing them nightly at the Meet & Greets, as I would escort the fan club members who won Meet & Greet passes.

This was one of my favorite tours I ever did with them. I would go out before every show and sell fan club memberships to the crowds of people that would line up, waiting to get in. I would give away Meet & Greet Passes or Happy Face Stickers (that allowed fans to dance on stage with them during the last song) or get fans in early to get to the front of the stage.

While this tour was an overall success for Destiny's Child, it wasn't a huge success for the fan club. We wanted to be selling a thousand memberships per night, and in reality, we were excited when we sold a few hundred. This wasn't a reflection on the ladies, as the sold-out shows were proof that their fan base was there—it was more about what we were selling: a fan club membership. Fans just didn't see the value in a membership. When I came back to the U.S. after this tour, I met with Mathew and told him my ideas for changing the way we did business with the fans.

I wanted to give the fans what they wanted, which was access to meet the ladies or at the very least to get an autograph as well as great tickets to the show, early access for general admission shows, etc. So instead of selling fan club memberships, I created a VIP Package for tour dates, which would include all the stuff that they wanted at a premium cost.

The first tour we sold these on was the Kelly Rowland solo European tour. They didn't sell out, but they sold enough to cover my cost of being on the road, which allowed me to take pictures and represent the fans and give them exclusive content from behind the scenes on tour.

Same with Beyoncé's first solo European tour in the fall of 2003. Popular enough to cover costs and make a small profit. By the Ladies First Tour in spring 2004, we were making a steady profit, which covered my touring costs and gave the fans what they wanted, plus it allowed me to be out on the road taking pictures nightly at the shows to get content for online and inter-acting with fans to ensure great customer service. I loved my job!

In the spring of 2005, we embarked on the Destiny Fulfilled and Lovin' It tour, which would become their final tour. It was quite memorable. I worked closely with Lauren Valencia, who was the McDonald's rep who traveled with us as the sponsor rep since McDonald's was the headlining sponsor. We were inseparable on that tour and had a lot of fun. We remained friends long after the tour was over. She sadly passed away in July 2019 of cancer.

We were in Australia and Destiny's Child rented a yacht to kick back and relax one night since we had the night off, and they invited the crew to join them. I had never been on a yacht before. I remember how fun it was to simply relax, instead of working around them. It was rare that I would take off my work hat around them, as I always felt like I had a job to do.

In summer of 2005 while on tour in Canada, there were death threats posted against me on the Destiny's Child message boards because I had denied a fan access to a Meet & Greet because he was obviously crazy. He was coming to the Canada shows, and Destiny's Child was concerned about my safety, so they assigned me security.

We had a lot of fun while touring. One night one of the camera operators, Redo, had lost his all-access laminate. As a joke, we made him wear a "Lil Bo-peep" hat that we made during the Denver show. He wore it all night, and when Kelly saw him from the stage she forgot the words that she was singing because she was laughing at how silly he looked. He was a good sport about it. There was always some prank or something funny going on backstage.

I remember going with Kelly to Lamar H.S. (which was my old high school). She surprised a group in the auditorium that was practicing singing. They presented her with an honorary diploma, I believe (if my memory serves), and we walked around the old campus. For me it was weird, because it was my high school too. They gave her a yearbook.

Later that day (or that week) we were in Baton Rouge at an

event, and I got called to the dressing room. The yearbook that they had given her was from my senior year of high school so I was in it a lot, and she saw me and freaked out—she had no idea we had gone to school together. We enjoyed looking through the yearbook together.

I remember when I went with Michelle to read to the kids—it was powerful as we drove because this was in March of 2006, I believe, and at least six months after Hurricane Katrina. Yet, as we drove to the event we were in awe at how much of the city was still destroyed and how very little was back to normal. I remember how sad it was.

We did an event once at the Houston Downtown Library where Kelly read to a group of kids. My sister came with me to the event, and I remember taking pictures of Kelly and the kids, etc. after she was finished. My sister wanted a picture, but unknown to me she asked Kelly if her sister could get in the photo, and Kelly said of course—only to have me have to hand the camera off to someone else—and Kelly was like—JENNETTE IS YOUR SISTER?!?!? LOL. In the photo, we were all laughing really big.

My favorite solo one-off event was getting to be at the "Crazy in Love" video shoot. I remember being nervous about going to the set of the video. I was there to escort two fans who were going to get to spend two days watching Beyoncé shoot the video. Here's a story I've never told anyone: When I arrived to the set, I was driving a red rental car. I parked a block away and walked, as I wasn't really sure where I was going. A few hours later, they were shooting the iconic opening scene where Beyoncé is walking down the street, and you can see my red rental car in the shot of the video. I was told that they were trying to locate

the driver (me) to move it, as they didn't want it in the shot ---
but I didn't know that at the time. I felt bad for ruining the shot.
But every time I see the video, I see my rental car and think
about that experience.

The ladies of Destiny's Child: Beyoncé, Kelly, and Michelle
are some of the most genuine and down-to-earth women you
will ever meet. The girls never turned down Make-A-Wish kids.
Any time they had a request from Make-A-Wish, we honored it,
and it was always so special to be a part of those moments. My
favorite moment was being present when Destiny's Child
presented their biggest fans with plaques at the end of the tour in
2005. It was so special, seeing these pop stars honor their fans in
such an amazing way. That's the genuine people that they are.
The plaques were personalized to each fan, with a message, and
signed and included a photo....

In late August 2005, I was called to their dressing room and
they told me that since this was their last tour—that they wanted
to do something special for specific fans that had been with them
all along. They named approximately fifteen fans and asked me
to coordinate getting plaques made for them, as well as making
sure that they were at the last shows (which most of them were
already planning on attending). They then invited the fans to the
Meet & Greets and surprised them with these huge two-foot by
three-foot plaques, each personalized with the fan's name and a
Meet & Greet photo from the tour. It was really sweet and
special, and was their genuine way of honoring their fans at the
end of their last tour. It was that same night in Seattle when I
asked to take a photo with them, and Beyoncé asked me to strike
a pose.

I couldn't think of anything, but the first thing that came to mind was the *Dreamgirls* pose, so we are all doing a *Dreamgirls* pose. We always had fun and were joking around like that.

It was also on this tour in September 2005 that we celebrated Beyoncé's birthday in Reno, Nevada. They rented this huge (I think famous from *The Big Lebowski*) bowling alley, and we had it all to ourselves after the show in Reno. We bowled and celebrated. Kelly and Michelle made Beyoncé go bowl with the few guys that were there—while they rehearsed with all the female dancers and crew, practicing a short dance to "Don't Cha" by the Pussycat Dolls. Beyoncé came in and all the females got up and danced on the top of the bar, just for her. It was so much fun and very memorable. I loved being a part of these real moments on tour.

Traveling on tour with them, the crew was my family. Destiny's Child surrounded themselves with amazing people on tour and I was lucky enough to be a part of their road family. There were touring rituals every night, with a prayer circle before going on stage. It wasn't just for the dancers and the band, but anyone who was part of the crew family could participate in the prayer circle each night. I found this to be so genuine, and it really was a family atmosphere out on the tour.

In November of 2005, I was able to go with them to the *Jimmy Kimmel Live!* taping, where they performed together for the last time as Destiny's Child. We did a special gathering for the fans, and it was truly special to see them one last time.

In 2006, I was able to travel to Los Angeles to be present for their Hollywood Walk of Fame Star Ceremony. It was pouring down rain, and I stood with their fans who had traveled to be there as well, and we were all drenched, but it felt like I was being a part of history in the making.

I treasured my time with them and would hope that if there was ever a reunion tour that I would get a phone call to make it back out on the road with them for old times' sake.

I'd like to think I had a very important role since I was the one in charge of interacting with their fans. I would activate the street teams and build the "BeyHive" so that when they were going to be on TRL with a new video, or when they would have a TV appearance—fans knew about it and were not only telling their friends but also calling in to vote their video higher on the countdown.

The fan base for them was truly homegrown and built from scratch. It grew quickly. When I started working with them we had about five hundred paying fan club members, and it was quickly at over ten thousand after about a year in 2001/2002. That was the *Survivor* album, and it was an anthem for a lot of people, including myself.

Their fan club members were amazing, especially the loyal fans from the jump: Elizabeth (Cherri), The Twins (Stacey and Tracey), Ricky, Tazmin, Laura, Jody, Jamie, Colyn, Elisabeth Moe in Norway, Rachel Crane, Mary O, Mary Heard, Rachel Mueller, Celine Hollenbeck, Delfine, Yuko Matsumoro, Dana Clark and Samantha Skone, and the hundreds more that I can't remember after all these years....

I don't remember there ever being a certain demographic that I was going after. I just went after their fans. Fans that I met on tour, fans that I met at events. I just took that personal meeting and expanded on it. I've always been a firm believer that once fans have met their favorite artist—if it was a positive experience, which I strived hard to make sure everyone always had—then you are building a lifetime fan. Those are the fans that will buy every album, see every show, and support everything you are doing as an artist because they've met the artist, and they feel like they are a part of it.

The rewards far outweighed the negatives. I got to travel the world and see some amazing places. I've been to forty-eight countries around the world, and almost all of my trips have been because of the ladies I worked for. I got to see the Eiffel Tower, hold a koala in Australia, go inside the Burj Al Arab Hotel (seven-star hotel in Dubai), visit Ethiopia, etc. Working with the girls as solo was easier, but not as much fun for me. I enjoyed working with Destiny's Child as a group more. It was easier to work with them solo because I only had to communicate with one person, versus three, and only track down one person to get autographs instead of three, etc.

It was also a different fan base, and I preferred the true Destiny's Child fans to any of the fans that I met while working with them individually. The Destiny's Child fans would come and support, but so would a lot of new people too. It was just different.

The single biggest obstacle the ladies had to overcome, I would say, were the rumors and the negative press. I hated hearing bad or negative things about them, or that they were backstabbing each other or being mean. I had the upmost respect for all of them because they were all such genuine, kind, and caring people that I hated when the media exploited them in a way that they could do nothing about. Because of the original members of the band leaving, and then Michelle and Farrah coming on board, and then Farrah leaving—it just gave the media good gossip to share, even when some of it wasn't true. I just hated watching that happen.

TAKEAWAYS...

Frank Gaston,

YOU KNOW, I HEAR PEOPLE SAY A LOT OF BAD THINGS ABOUT Mathew Knowles, but he's so important to that group. It's just the dedication, the not having the big budgets at first, the working really hard. I think the sad thing about Mathew is that he became a superstar himself. I don't think he ever expected that part of it. I remember this man who hustled. Kind of reminds me of myself right now with my girl group. I learned from him how to be relentless, he really had to do it himself; he couldn't depend on someone else to do it because they didn't believe in the girls like that.

My takeaway with Destiny's Child, and the Jackson 5, I have to say is: groups that have their parents as the managers are the most successful groups in the world because parents are unconditionally gonna do what they have to do. That's my takeaway. So if you can get somebody who acts like your dad or mom, that's important to a group's success, especially with black groups. If you go on record and think about all the biggest groups in the world that were black and successful—like the Jackson 5 and Destiny's Child, I would want my group to be like that because I feel like I'm their dad.

You know, we're driving around in an SUV, and everybody's got a big 'ole bus on this Xscape tour, and I know Matt's done the same thing. He would be in some little truck and the girls would be leaning on one another with their rollers in their hair, and Mrs. Tina would be on the other side, and everybody else had these big old buses. But they did what they had to do, so that's sacrifice. The family part of it is so important. That's my takeaway.

Dwayne Wiggins

Those are things I had to learn. Sometimes it's better being behind the scenes because you run things better. I also learned to be a good leader, and that you have to be a good follower. You have to know how to listen. I learned so much from that group. Mathew took my game to a tremendous level. Tina, she was icing on the cake when I finally went to Houston and I saw they had their own family business.

That's the reason I came back and started my cafe with my family. The Java House in '99. When I finally got a chance to see them and what they did up there, I came home and I was like, "I'm not opening up no fucking club. My daughter and my wife and all of us, we're working together." Like I said, it's just the experience that you get from people that helps you grow.

One last memory is from the time when they would come

over to the house. I remember them holding my son, who was at the time like six, seven months old, not quite a year.

We were all there in the kitchen with them holding onto him and going, "Go Dylan, Go Dylan." I gotta find that tape we made of it. But he now is producing, and he just produced Solange! So they're all in the business. They've only been exposed to this shit. That's the only way they know how to do it.

Arne Frager

I've got a funny attitude toward the record industry, and I feel like if I do something, and it has merit, I will do well with it, and then later on the group does well, but I didn't have anything to do with their success. I don't want to try and milk it and make money off it. I knew myself that I could have released that record, and I think I could have probably made a lot of money when Beyoncé became such a big star, but I just didn't feel good about that. And so one day I thought, well, what am I going to do? I've got all this content ... somebody is going to want to release this someday because Beyoncé's become an international star and rightfully so. So then I offered it to Mathew.

I've never done anything with the Girls Tyme stuff except follow Beyoncé in the trades and be thrilled for her. A great thing to kind of close out on is your integrity and how you treat the industry because so many people are exploiting. The most exciting thing I've ever done, whether I made money with that project or not, is to work with a completely unknown person who doesn't have any real connections in the industry or a lot of money.

You help them get somewhere and then they blow up and

become a real international star, and they make millions of dollars—you just feel like wow, I really made a contribution to someone's life, and you got to feel good about that.

Linda Ragland

What I would like to say at this point, and I knew this while I was there, honestly Destiny's Child would not have made it without Mathew Knowles, and that is just the truth. I'm speaking from a business and a strategic point of view, and having an ear for music. You know—all kind of rumors are floating around about his personal life and all of that.

So that's that. But when it comes to who made this group what it is, it was Mathew Knowles. I was there in that office when many decisions had to be made, and many were not just contractual decisions but decisions about what song needed to go on an album, who needed to produce. Rodney Jerkins, pulling these producers in when they weren't even super producers at that time, but just knowing. I witnessed him making these girls great. I really did.

Kim Burse

Whether you got paid for it or not. Just from your inner spirit you knew the right thing to do was to fight for those girls, and fight for them to have a chance and an avenue to be what they would ultimately be in life and in society and in this world. Even after spending so many years creating so many shows, so many musical arrangements, I am grateful for being a part of the girls' success.

I recently saw Beyoncé at the Rose Bowl. We got to sit down and talk for ten minutes, which was good, as I hadn't seen her in some years.

It was just so gratifying to know that this girl really got her chance to be a superstar. God bless Mathew because he not only pushed the road, paved it, swept it, made sure there were cars running on both sides, right. He had to be the manager and dad that he was to make sure that train never stopped. I'm just so grateful to have had the opportunity to even be a passenger on the train and to be a part of it and to be a part of it from somewhat of the beginning of it, you know?

There's so many things that have stemmed from it for my life that that's its own the story as well. Congratulations to Teresa too, because she's still with Beyoncé, and she was the lady who basically found what may have been considered a diamond in the rough back then. She's still with her, and that speaks volumes as well, to know that she's been at this girl's side for every musical project, professional musical project that she's done.

There's a lot of rich history, a lot of rich history, and I'm glad Mathew's doing this to, like he said to me, he wants to be the one to tell the story to make sure it gets told right because if he doesn't tell this story somebody else will, and it won't be right.

Mathew Knowles

Just as the group Destiny's Child didn't retire, neither did the rest of us. I certainly didn't see them going on into individual projects and family life for a while as any sort of ending, and neither did they. Music World Entertainment continues as a premier record label, and many of the staff members such as

Anissa Gordon and others remain a vital part of the engine. Several of the administrative and creative teams continue to work with Beyoncé, and solo projects continue for them all.

Many of the former group members have had their ups and downs, but how proud I am to see so many ups, such as LeToya's acting career, which is stellar. Careers and names have been built from what started out as Girls Tyme, a small Houston-based group of pre-teen girls, to Destiny's Child—the world's most successful girl's group.

I was a pivotal part of that and have no regrets about those obstacles and challenges that met us along the way. Despite the scandals and the misperceptions surrounding our journey, we all worked our asses off just to keep the music coming—whether as executives making it happen, or the talent creating the magic.

I've been called every name imaginable, but what this business has taught me is that what people call you is based on your current circumstance. One come-up in a new direction can have everybody singing your name, one trip down and nobody knows your name. What lasts is what is written in blood, like the name "father." What holds out is legacy, like the name "manager of the world's most successful girl group." You can hang your hat on those.

When I look back over that long road, I see we created a better life for the next generation. Our hardships stayed in the past. While the young ladies' personal hardships were their own, they were nothing like the economic scraping-by their fore-parents knew. They all found their voices at a young age and carried their dreams into adulthood—motherhood. They grew up, they blew up, and the rest is supposed to be history. But as we see through so many personal oral histories, every angle had not been told. Not all of the conversations around Destiny's Child were finished. Yet, life moved on, and so did the music. Tina and I found wonderful new marriages and salvaged a friendship, and are now co-parenting and grandparenting happily.

"Destiny" literally means the hidden power controlling what will happen in the future: fate. I can't see the future, I only aim for what I want it to be. Yet looking over the past, I see the hidden power. I see the push where it was needed, and the pull when they became wanted by the world. I look at where we started on the journey and see them now... living the fabulous fate of destiny fulfilled.

THE ALBUM

DESTINY'S CHILD: THE UNTOLD STORY PRESENTS GIRLS TYME

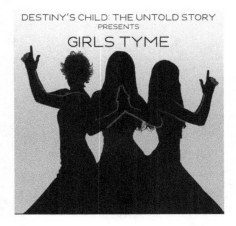

BEFORE THE ICONIC SUPER GIRL GROUP DESTINY'S CHILD there was Girls Tyme. Formed in Houston, TX in the early 1990s, the tween singing group was led by the Queen Bey herself, Beyoncé Knowles, alongside Kelly Rowland, LaToya Luckett, LaTavia Roberson, Prince protégé Ashley "Tamar" Davis, and sisters Nina and Nikki Taylor.

The group's manager and mastermind, music executive Mathew Knowles, has uncovered a never before released album called *Destiny's Child: The Untold Story Presents Girls Tyme.*

Produced by Arne Frager and Alonzo Jackson, the album is a funky playful mix of R&B tunes that offers the listener a glimpse into the early stages of Destiny's Child.

Get Your Copy
http://www.mathewknowles.com

ALSO BY MATHEW KNOWLES

DNA of Achievers

Racism from the Eyes of a Child

The Emancipation of Slaves Through Music

Public Relations and Media

Destiny's Child: The Untold Story

ABOUT MATHEW KNOWLES

Mathew Knowles is an award-winning music executive and CEO of Music World Entertainment, which successfully managed and produced such acts as Destiny's Child and Beyoncé, among others. He is a 1974 graduate of Fisk University in Nashville, Tennessee, where he earned both a Bachelor of Arts degree in Economics and a Bachelor of Science degree in Business Administration. He earned his M.B.A. and Ph.D. from Cornerstone Christian and Bible College. Knowles is currently a professor at Prairie View A&M, where he teaches Sports, Events, and Entertainment Marketing.

Knowles is the recipient of the Century Award of Excellence (1911–2011) from the Omega Psi Phi fraternity. He also received the 2011 Living Legends Foundation Award and was named the "2007 International Executive of the Year" by the Greater Houston Partnership. Knowles is an active and longtime voting member of the National Academy of Recording Arts and Sciences (NARAS) and served on its GRAMMY Board Committee. In 2011, he was appointed to the Board of Directors of the Gospel Music Association. For information regarding bookings for speaking go to: Mathewknowles.com

CPSIA information can be obtained
at www.ICGtesting.com
Printed in the USA
LVHW091136100120
643221LV00001B/232/P